CHINESE ROOTS

Printed in Australia
Cover design by Shawline Publishing Group Pty Ltd
Images in this book are copyright approved for Shawline Publishing Group Pty Ltd
Illustrations within this book are copyright approved for Shawline Publishing Group Pty Ltd

First Printing: March 2023
Shawline Publishing Group Pty Ltd
www.shawlinepublishing.com.au

Paperback ISBN 978-1-9228-5175-8
eBook ISBN 978-1-9228-5181-9

Distributed by Shawline Distribution and Lightningsource Global

A catalogue record for this
work is available from the
National Library of Australia

More great Shawline titles can be found here:

New titles also available through Books@Home Pty Ltd.
Subscribe today - www.booksathome.com.au

CHINESE ROOTS

YVONNE HORSFIELD

This book is dedicated in loving memory to my mother,
Nancy Evelyn Lidgerwood (nee Way) and my grandfather,
Hedley David Way.

Acknowledgements

This story has been researched and written, largely based upon my childhood experiences and cherished family memorabilia, plus oral interviews with members of the family. My second cousin, Michael Way contributed generously with his own research to get me started. The completion of this book is due to the promise I made my mother on her death bed.

4 GENERATIONS OF TONGWAY FAMILY IN AUSTRALIA

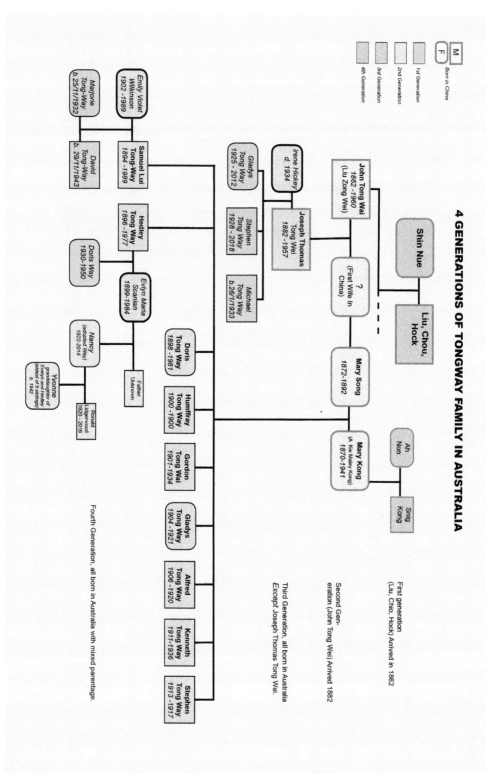

First generation
(Liu, Chio, Hock) Arrived in 1862

Second Gen-
eration (John Tong Wei) Arrived 1882

Third Generation, all born in Australia
Except Joseph Thomas Tong Wei.

Fourth Generation, all born in Australia with mixed parentage.

CONTENTS

INTRODUCTION

I t is strange how rare instances arise in life, when one can be struck with a moment of clarity in which you are foretold of an event. I recall that day in January when I took my leave of him as if it has been etched upon my brain. I fastened my seatbelt and accelerated, giving one last wave of my hand as I gazed into the rear vision mirror with the consciousness of a dull ache rising within me. Unasked, the tears began to course slowly down my cheeks as the slender, frail figure of that small, solitary old man gradually disappeared before my eyes. He stood, the last one of his family's generation, hugging the edge of the pavement until I vanished from view.

I drove on mechanically, not noticing the road or where I was going, nor very much caring. Swamped with an inexplicable sense of loss, I somehow understood deep in my bones that I would never meet him again. The pain of this moment swept over me, sharpened by the recognition that our brief and precious time together was over. For quite some time I continued blindly, until finally the newness of the roadside scenery registered. I was in unfamiliar territory and must have taken a wrong turn off the main highway from Bendigo. To my surprise, I found myself near the small town of Malmsbury, even though I had travelled this route back home to Ballarat many times before without mishap. I was miles out of the way from my normal route, but it gave me time to compose my thoughts and relive some of those precious moments which are now indelibly recorded upon my memory. Later on, as I mulled over the events of this last visit, I asked myself what it was that had triggered this premonition of Uncle Sam's death.

Yes, he had been more relaxed and less formal with me than ever before! He had greeted me with a handshake when he answered the door as was his custom, but this time, he was eager to know that my story of the family history which included his own recollections and memorabilia had been completed. For a man of 92 he was still amazingly agile and sprightly of mind and body, with a smooth skin and youthful appearance which much belied his age. When young, he had always been considered the good looking one, despite his 'Asian' features. Almost eagerly he received the folder of the family history I gave him and settled himself down at the dining room table, beckoning for me to sit in the adjacent chair.

With an air of great solemnity and purpose, he took his spectacles from their case, placed them upon his nose and proceeded to open the folder. In silence, as if time had been suspended and we were the actors in a slow-motion movie, he began to read each page, occasionally stopping to remark on some minor detail of information he considered to be not accurate enough and which required alteration. I had not expected such a dedicated application to the task in hand, but he read the entirety of it in one sitting from cover to cover, before he looked up to pass judgement.

'I must congratulate you for an excellent piece of work! There are just those few details you will need to correct,' he said in his formal schoolteacher's voice. Of course, he was referring to a few alterations mainly in reference to himself, Samuel John Tongway. He held a notion of himself as a worthy Australian-born Chinese who was legitimised by the lifelong achievements in which he had distinguished himself as a respectable citizen, retired headmaster and pillar of conservative society. He was particularly proud of the fact that he had been the only First World War veteran to march on Anzac Day in Bendigo recently and he eagerly displayed to me the newspaper excerpt he had kept from an item on the front page of the *Bendigo Advertiser*. In his eyes he was 'whiter than white', and considered that he had earned the right to regard himself as such.

Basking in the glow of this rare moment of approval and sensing that I had come through the formal barrier of politeness in which he'd long held me at arm's length over a two-year period of scrutiny, I was gratified and relieved to have emerged relatively unscathed. After sharing a cup of tea together with the scones I had baked him, he varied normal procedure from the usual polite observance in which he took his formal farewell of me with a handshake at the front door. Uncharacteristically, he had decided to accompany me to my car, parked out front on the roadway. I was acutely conscious that the purpose for my visits under the pretext of family research no longer existed. We stood a little awkwardly on the footpath before saying our goodbyes; he took my hand to shake it, then for the first time simultaneously kissed me on the cheek, as if on a sudden impulse. This was the moment of my demise! The significance of this brief unbending slowly dawned upon me and a mutual realisation passed between us at that moment – he had known it also; a premonition that this was to be our final goodbye.

Since then, the poignancy of those few precious meetings I had snatched so late in his long life of 92 years have haunted and reminded me of those wasted, tragic years which have plagued and fragmented my family for so long. It tempered my resolve to unravel and reclaim these fragments; to piece them together like the smashed sections of one of my grandmother's treasured Chinese bowls, for these fragments are all she was finally left with and they are the symbols of a legacy I was born into. I resolved to make some sense of these fragments of their lives by recording their individual stories, by putting the pieces back together in the hope of resolution and to restore a sense of connection with the past, once divided by two opposing cultures and differing loyalties. Their epitaph lies in unyielding stone at the Ballarat Cemetery in mute testimony to the stories sealed within and never told.

It is my hope that the long-cherished and -remembered Chinese proverb will be fulfilled by this telling of our family story:

'Upon the roots of the tree rest falling leaves.'

TSIN CHIN SHAN – FIRST GENERATION

The story begins during the early gold rush discoveries which heralded the great influx of eager immigrants to Victoria from mid-1851. Following on the heels of the Europeans came the first shiploads of Chinese gold seekers, their numbers swelling rapidly in the frenzy of feverish acquisition and hard labour which spread like the tentacles of a hidden virus throughout the colony, filling the headlines of newspapers at home and abroad.

1. Line drawing of Chinese by Garth

It was in this climate that Liu Chou Hock, a peasant farmer from the village of Wang Tung in the province of Kwangtung, joined the many gold-seekers in 1863, who years before him had rushed to gain indentured passage to Victoria from money lenders, and departed from Hong Kong.

2. Photo of village - Wang Tung 2018

It was the first time he was to leave his wife, Shin Nue, and his infant son, Liu Zong Wei, to venture far beyond the confines of the village, traveling on foot with other men from the Sze Yap district of Toishan in south-western Kwangtung. The journey to reach Canton took three days, with each member traveling at a trot in single file so as not to entangle the loaded baskets or ta'ams they were carrying, carefully balanced across their shoulders. Upon reaching the ancient, walled city of Canton, their destination was the Pearl River on the southern side of the city. The water's edge was crowded with the river junks which were to carry them, jammed together like sardines, bound for the port of Hong Kong in readiness for the time of their departure to the promised land of Tsin Chin Shan, or New Gold Mountain.

Along the way, their eyes captured the scenes of life on the riverbanks and beyond, with the distant villages and farmhouse plantations of mulberry trees, sugar cane and clumps of bamboo and fruit orchards. On the river itself were fisher folk busy hauling and plundering the fish from their coarse bamboo nets, surrounded by the rich multitude of bird life such as the wild fowl, ducks, geese, coots and other river birds which provided the food source and livelihoods of so many. Down river they passed the great sea-going junks, decorated with huge wooden heads of dragons. Strains of music were heard from passing flower boats. There were the brightly coloured revenue cruisers, armed with flashing cannons and flying large flags painted with vermillion characters to distinguish them from lesser vessels. It was all a fascinating sight for Liu Chou Hock and his companions who had never witnessed such an amazing variety of life and activity before in their simple village existences.

As the junk entered the western channel of the Hong Kong harbour, the spirits of even the most despondent villager must have risen to admire the beauty of Victoria Peak in the background, bathed in morning sunshine. The calm waters of the harbour were filled with shipping and familiar sampans; lorchas and junks were overshadowed by the men of war and merchant ships of many nations. In contrast with the relative discomfort of the junk they had travelled in for the last leg of their river journey, upon reaching their destination, the accommodation they faced in the Hong Kong barracoon enclosures was more primitive than holding pens for animals waiting for slaughter. Their conditions were squalid, vermin infested and drastically overcrowded: the doors were heavily padlocked to prevent escape and the windows were boarded and nailed so little light could penetrate the interior. The makeshift sanitation was grossly inadequate, and the only food supplied was a bowl of rice, sometimes with a bit of salted cabbage. Held within this virtual prison, many were induced to gamble and often borrow money they could ill afford to repay, or they were persuaded to dull their senses with opium to endure the anxiety of waiting. Despite many who regretted their plight and looked for escape, this was where they were to remain until their departure for Australia and, along with his companions, Lue Chou Hock was forced to endure it the best he could manage.

Finally, they were informed that their waiting was over. On boarding the vessel, they were lined up on deck for inspection and the counting of heads. This was to be the only time they were permitted to enjoy daylight and fresh air for the duration of the voyage. When standing on the ship's deck as it readied for departure, Liu Chou Hock was to gaze back at the shoreline of his native land with mingled thoughts and emotions; of regret at the way in which he had forsaken his young wife, Shin Nue, and his only firstborn infant son, barely two years of age. But as he ventured into the unknown, there was also hope, mingled with apprehension and excitement which rose in his throat as he contemplated the opportunity which promised him chances of reward. He thought of the honour it could bring to him and his family on a successful return from Tsin Chin Shan, the New Gold Mountain he hoped to reach, known as Australia. Whilst he gazed into the endless waves before him, he knew that if the fates willed it thus, the god of wealth would be bountiful, and luck would be on his side. He was still young and strong from a life of tilling the soil in the small plot of land which for generations had belonged to his family in the village of Wang Tung in the Sze Yap district. Furthermore, he had only to support two mouths to feed, because his aged parents had already joined their ancestors in the great spirit world. He felt confident that he would be able to send enough home from his earnings to support them until his return. On that, his honour depended, and he had made a pledge. Dutifully, his wife had submitted to his will, but he had heard much wailing and sorrow expressed behind closed doors at the time of his departure.

Thus, it was that travelling steerage class in the hold of a ship, jam packed to overflowing with Chinese gold seekers like himself, he endured the privations of the journey with appalling sanitation, poor drinking water, and food unfit for normal human consumption. Added to this, the months of interminable sea sickness and the inescapable, close bodily proximity to other sufferers; some of whom succumbed to fevers and illness brought on by their living conditions. Sadly, it was they who were not destined to see the shores of Tsin

Chin Shan, let alone return to their homeland. So many of them were illiterate peasants who could neither read nor write, hence their fate went unrecorded and consumed by the ocean, their plight remaining forever unknown back home.

Fortunately for Liu Chou Hock, he was able to doggedly endure the privations of the journey and after his embarkation at the Port of Melbourne, he made his way on foot towards Ballarat with many others of his countrymen from the Sze Yap district. Travelling through Flemington and on to Digger's Rest where they rested overnight, they made an unusual sight moving in a single procession with heavily loaded bamboo ta'ams across their shoulders and traveling with surprising swiftness in their customary shuffling gait to conserve energy. On reaching Ballarat, Liu Chou Hock eventually staked out a claim and with a few fellow villagers, he concentrated on reworking many of the early abandoned sites which still offered rich pickings for the patient, hard-working Chinese. These men worked diligently and were prepared to carefully pan, sluice, cradle and thoroughly reprocess the mullock and dirt from the leftovers of earlier miners whose frenzy for easy pickings meant that their methods had been slapdash and much alluvial gold and even small nuggets had been overlooked.

Eventually, Liu Chou Hock concentrated on the outer goldfields situated miles from Ballarat, such as Smythesdale, Scarsdale and Haddon, where although the surface gold had run out, a new phase of deep lead mining had begun. This occurred with rich deposits being discovered underground and the opportunity for small shareholders with some capital to invest in local company mines or contracted to work as tributors in small groups for the larger mines. Hence, there were a few Chinese like himself who were able to reap the benefits of their hard-earned effort from their savings and earlier back-breaking work. Unlike some of his countrymen who succumbed to the loneliness and feelings of homesickness, he did not while away the hours by gambling at Fan Tan and smoking the opium pipe to dull the senses. Liu was carefully putting aside the profits he made and sending what he could spare back home to repay his debt for the indentured journey; the remainder being sent and entrusted to his wife and family in the village of Wang Tung. There was no opportunity for any social contact with the white European community in the local area, because their Chinese camp was well separated from the dwellings of the remaining inhabitants. This suited Liu Chou Hock and his fellow countrymen, who were aware of European resentment against their cultural differences and their modest mining successes on the fields. He was proud of his own ancient land, and he regarded these recent usurpers of the lands of the New Gold Mountain from the indigenous Aboriginal people as the true, uncultivated 'barbarians'.

He worked steadfastly for almost a three-year period until he considered he had been successful enough to book his passage and return to China in the knowledge that he was now a wealthy man in the eyes of all in the village who knew him. Unlike many less fortunate others amongst his countrymen, Liu was able to return home with honour and claim the prestige which gold discovery had bestowed upon him. In this way his newfound wealth enabled him to consider how he could provide a better life and future for his family, especially for Liu Zong Wei, the young son he had left behind at two years of age. What a difference these foreign years of toil had made to the family fortunes. For his wife, he was now able to build a bigger and better home and he would ensure that this money was wisely invested, because it provided the means for educating his son, now five years of age. Education and scholastic ability were highly valued in China and the sole means by which the youths of the village could obtain social mobility via the annual public service exams: success could secure high ranking positions attached to government and possibly ensure a lifestyle of greater affluence and security for his son, plus increased status for the entire family. Also, young Liu Zong Wei viewed his father as an enlightened man and free thinker for his time, as he explained many years later in his memoirs, 'My father was a follower of Confucius and he was very anxious that I should have a good education and be thoroughly instructed in the teachings of Confucius'. Unlike many others in the village, his father failed to entertain the superstitious beliefs and religious practices associated with the Joss, commonly held by his wife and their fellow villagers. Therefore, Liu Zong Wei became proficient in the teachings of Confucius, in line with his own father's wishes and beliefs. Unlike the majority of children in the village who were the offspring of poor peasant farmers eking out the barest subsistence living from their rice crops, Liu Zong Wei regularly attended school, with the intention that he would eventually become a successful scholar whom his mother and father could be extremely proud of. Between the ages of eight to twelve years, he had mastered all the principal books of Confucius that were taught and at thirteen years he subsequently continued with his college education in a neighbouring village until, at eighteen years old, he finally gained an appointment as the village schoolmaster.

SECOND GENERATION GOLD SEEKER

As manhood approached, Liu Zong Wei dutifully fulfilled his marital obligation to marry the young Chinese woman his parents had selected for him. They had arranged a good dowry price from her parents since early childhood, as was customary in Chinese traditional society. Soon after their marriage, his wife gave birth to a healthy son and thus, the pattern of his future comfortable and respectable life seemed assured. However, during the two years he had worked as a school master, he had become restless and, despite his good fortune, he was troubled with the tempting thoughts of his father's earlier adventures in a far-off land when about his own age. He was fascinated by his father's stories that he had told and retold to his son over so many years during his youth: of how his father had travelled to Tsin Chin Shan and witnessed all the wonders and curiosities of this new land. It was a land that promised riches and new, exciting prospects to those fellow gold seekers like his father, who came from all walks of life and from many different cultures and countries throughout the world. He had been told about incredible, new inventions such as the miraculous sending of messages across the ocean to distant lands by means of wires; it teased at his imagination with the desire to know more.

By the time Liu Zong Wei was 22 years of age, despite the security of his family life and the birth of a new young son he was proud of, ultimately, he could resist the temptation to follow in his father's footsteps no longer. Gold mining and new discoveries continued to lure young Chinese men to seek their fortunes on the Victorian goldfields of this new land called Australia and there were many of his countrymen still returning successfully with incredible stories of their experiences and good fortune. He was also keen to see the amazing inventions his father had spoken of when he was growing up, with wonderful railways, booming goldmines, and those incredible telegraph systems. Years later he reminisced, 'Not believing that half the wonderful things were true, I decided to come and see for myself. The idea that a man in England could speak to a man in Hong Kong along wires upheld by poles and through cables under the sea and get an answer back in a few hours, was to my mind utterly absurd.'

Despite the tears and pleading of his wife and family, nor the efforts his father made to dissuade him, he could not be deterred from his resolve to go. He was warned by his father of the hardships of the journey, of the many village men who did not return, of the physical risks that mining presented in the form of hard labour and the many accidents which could occur. He was also reminded that his comfortable life as a village school master did not prepare him for the conditions he would be forced to endure. None of these good arguments prevailed, because his mind was made up.

Unlike his father before him, he was able to pay his passage without obligation to village money lenders or his parents. Taking his leave of the family and all well-wishers in the village, he travelled to Hong Kong where he arranged his ship's passage on the *Hungarian* travelling in steerage class. He boarded and set sail from Hong Kong on 4th October 1882 with high spirits and the anticipation of adventure in his heart. Neither the common hardships of the journey nor the risks he was taking had any effect on the sense of purpose he experienced and which sustained him over the following weeks at sea. With high hopes, he arrived in the Port of Melbourne none the worse for his long voyage. He was quite heedless of the strange sight he must have presented to the majority of Victorians and non-Chinese arrivals as he disembarked, with his closely shaven forehead and the long, braided queue still trailing down his back and his traditional, loose, blue, cotton Chinese garments. Unlike the majority of Chinese men most European people were accustomed to seeing, he was very erect and tall and did not carry his belongings in the ta'am baskets balanced across the shoulders. Instead, he carried a woven cloth bag which contained all his essential belongings. He walked differently, without the customary shuffle that accompanied those men who were used to tilling the soil and bearing heavy loads since childhood. Also, Liu Zong Wei was not accustomed to any acknowledgement of inferiority amongst men of different cultures, and therefore he was blissfully unaware of the need for deference when not with his own kind in this strange land.

As a measure of convenience, from now on he decided to adopt the name of John Tong Wai and forgo the family's clan name of Liu, matching the same way it had already been entered on his passport. John appeared to be the common first name used for most Chinese as it was easier for non-Chinese strangers to understand, especially when it was necessary to put it into writing. Retracing his father's footsteps, thankfully he was able to join with several other Chinese travellers who were making their way to the goldfields of the Ballarat district which it was reputed, still had a plentiful supply of gold from the deep lead deposits currently being mined. As well, there were the larger Company mines which extracted the gold from the many quartz reefs deep underground. John was intent on traveling to the Ballarat district in the hope that good fortune still smiled upon the family, making his way to a place called Haddon not too far away. Here, he knew that an uncle of his was already mining a claim with some success. He understood that several months before, his uncle had been sent a message of his possible arrival at Haddon during 1883, which had been transmitted from the Sze Yap society in Melbourne. Most of his countrymen in Victoria had joined the membership of this Chinese society for the deemed benefits of fellowship, guidance and protection of their welfare in this strange new place.

Following an arduous and dusty journey along the common route from the docks of Melbourne, through Flemington, and on towards the distant outpost of Digger's Rest, they camped here for the night, sleeping on bed rolls laid out on bare ground. They continued next day towards Bacchus Marsh, a small settlement which lay in a fertile river valley, surrounded by steep mountains. At this stage, they decided to shorten their journey and avoid the strenuous climb over the Pentland Range ahead of them by purchasing a rail ticket to Ballarat, stopping overnight and departing from the Border Inn the next morning. Nevertheless, the journey still took several hours, and the train was filled to capacity, with John and his Chinese companions aboard. Perhaps by good fortune, it appeared that there were not many other European passengers choosing to travel on this particular voyage, so they were not subjected to many curious or unfriendly stares from other non-Chinese. As they neared Ballarat, two distinguishing outlines of the twin volcanic cones of Mount Warrengeep (Warrenheip) and Mount Boninyowang (Buninyong) appeared on the horizon, looming ever larger before their gaze as they neared their destination.

John made his way from the Ballarat station to where there were horse-drawn vehicles lined up near Craig's Grand Hotel with the laneway leading to Bath's Stables in the rear. He was now faced with the task of finding the whereabouts of his uncle's claim at this place called Haddon. He decided to share the cost and accompany the others, travelling by carriage to the Chinese camp situated along Main Road and further up the hillside at a place called Golden Point, overlooked by the Presbyterian Chinese Mission Church on Young Street. He was told by the coachman to visit the Manse next door to the church where the superintendent missioner, Reverend James Chue, administered to the spiritual and practical needs of the Chinese and who would be able to advise him as to the best way of reaching his uncle.

3. *Rev. James Chue*

On his arrival, John stepped onto the front veranda of the wooden house and knocked on the front door. It opened to meet a smiling, round, Asian face: the man he presumed to be Reverend Chue, who was dressed as a typical clergyman in a round white collar and a black suit. He was received in a kindly manner by Reverend Chue, who invited him to rest on a chair in the front room. Upon hearing of John's need to find the whereabouts of his uncle at Haddon, he immediately sent a messenger to arrange for John to travel by horse and cart in company with a Chinese man by the name of Lo Kwoi Sang, a herbalist who had a successful herbal practice in nearby Peel Street.

4. Lo Kwoi Sang

When he arrived, Mr Sang told John that sometimes he delivered his potions to Haddon and other Chinese camps where his patients were located and when they had become too ill to visit him. Proudly, Lo Kwoi Sang also told John in conversation that he was a doctor with a medical background, having studied and qualified in Edinburgh and later he became a surgeon in the Chinese Navy. When he first came to Australia, he travelled as ship's surgeon on the barque named *Eliza Jane*, arriving in July 1871. He told John that already, in the Ballarat district, he had established a good reputation as a skilled herbalist and medical man situated in the busy heart of the goldfield, which ensured him a good livelihood, whereby he found it unnecessary to stoop to the hardships of mining. Fortunately for John, Lo Kwoi Sang had knowledge of his uncle and the whereabouts of his claim. At some stage John's uncle had been one of his patients, along with the many other Chinese miners who came to him with their ailments. Accidents were also common, so Lo Kwoi Sang's former experience as a ship's surgeon was put to good use many times. He had met up with objections from the medical fraternity of Ballarat, who had complained to the medical board because he used the title of 'doctor', but he had strongly resisted these pressures and insisted on retaining the right to call himself a qualified medical man due to his many successful treatments and the written testimonials of his satisfied patients printed in the local newspaper. He claimed to have cured many of his patients confined in the early stages of Diphtheria with a special herbal preparation he made up. He explained to John that he had made enough money to send to his village in China for his family's regular support and unless he could find a respectable woman who would marry him in the near future, he planned to make enough in order to pay for his passage back home to China permanently. He repeated to John the contents of the well-known Chinese proverb:

'Upon the roots of the tree rest falling leaves.'

At this stage of his journey, John had no intention of heeding these sentiments, but he was glad to have already made a friend that he could call on whilst in the Haddon district.

Lo Kwoi Sang drove the cart to a boggy row of claims not far from the Chinese camp beside what was once a clear, running stream, but now a muddy quagmire. It was surrounded by a multitude of Chinese men absorbed with the effort of cradling, shovelling, and processing mounds of dirt dug from the nearby shallow shafts. By a row of dirty, bedraggled canvas tents and a few crude huts, Lo Kwoi Sang called to one of the men and bowed his head several times, with hands customarily pressed together beneath his chin in polite greeting. At last John was made known to his uncle, who responded with similar greetings, exuding an air of excitement upon every feature of his round, smiling, careworn face. Taking his leave of his newfound friend, John thanked Lo Kwoi Sang, who was eager to return to his own dwelling in Ballarat before dark. The primitive conditions John was to live and work under, he was already beginning to take in, with the realisation that his father's warnings had not been exaggerated. However, his uncle was pleased to have an extra pair of hands to help him with the physical work, which would now be shared with the other members of the claim who politely put aside their labours and joined in to make him welcome.

The following days flowed into weeks and John soon realised his short comings: that he was not as enthusiastic or able to put up with the agonising hard labour and daily repetition of tasks amongst the dirt and damp conditions in the endless pursuit of those elusive gold deposits as were the rest of his party. His Uncle became impatient with him, because he worked slowly and did not show enough enthusiasm, even when the glitter of alluvial gold made an appearance before his eyes in either the panning dish or the wooden cradle.

John soon found himself put onto the lighter duties of cooking and preparing most of the meals. It was whilst around the campfire chopping up some of the vegetables that they had grown in a plot of ground nearby, that John received an unexpected visit from a strange Chinese man. He was not dressed in their customary, traditional loose clothing and he was without a queue, wearing a black broad-brimmed hat and dark clothing as often worn by a non-Chinese gentleman. He introduced himself as Mr. Lue Cheong and explained that he was representing the true Christian faith with the word of God. In his work as a catechist for the Wesleyan Church, his mission was to convert 'new souls' and train other catechists who would spread the Christian faith amongst his fellow Chinese countrymen and 'lead them to the true light of God'. John listened with interest, as he was impressed by the educated demeanour of this man and also by his earnestness and sincerity. Lue Cheong spoke to him of the true word represented in the Bible which gave the message of love for our fellow man and the forgiveness of our worldly sins from Jesus Christ our Saviour. He invited John to visit him in his tent on the edge of the mining township that evening for further discussion and stories from the Bible. When darkness fell, John absented himself from the camp and made his way to Lue Cheong's tent, which was easy to identify by the wooden crucifix which stood aloft of the hut roofline. He was curious to hear a bit more from this interesting new acquaintance.

It was to be the first of many visits and the cementing of a firm friendship between the two men who recognised that they were equals in education and enthusiastic to learn and spread the message of Jesus to the remainder of the Chinese community around them. During their meetings, John was taught to join with Lue Cheong in singing the hymns of praise and joy associated with the Wesleyan Church. He invited John to join him in the Wesleyan services and continue his visits for further instruction. However, it was not long before John's uncle became suspicious of his evening disappearances and he questioned John, asking him where he was going so frequently; perhaps in fear of him visiting the sly grog shanty or the opium dens where some unfortunates who were homesick or down on their luck ended up as a solace for their woes. John assured him that this was not so, but he was then compelled to confess his friendship with Lue Cheong and the reason for his nightly visits. His uncle immediately broke into a rage and beat him with a raised stick, loudly accusing him of being a 'Foolish Jesus Fellow' and chasing him around the camp. As John later recalled in his diary, he then suffered 'much persecution' from his fellow countrymen and his uncle threatened to 'have him drowned' if he continued with his folly! It was this incident that made up John's mind that he could not tolerate the vicissitudes of mining any longer and he packed his few belongings before seeking out his uncle at the claim and telling him that he was going to seek work 'spreading the word of the gospel' with Mr. Lue Cheong, his friend. His uncle was screaming abuse and threw clods of earth at him in fury as he departed unceremoniously and with great haste from the camp. He found Lue Cheong reading in his hut and explained that he wished to help him spread the word of Jesus among his fellows, who presently worshipped only heathen Gods at the local Joss House. Lue Cheong was delighted to have an assistant and hastened to introduce him to Reverend Mr William Youngman who had formerly been an early missionary to the Chinese population in Singapore.

5. Reverend William Youngman and wife

The Wesleyans had already established a Chinese Mission church at Castlemaine and in 1860 a new mission was also established in Ballarat under the care of Reverend Youngman, who had trained the first converts, many of whom became catechists to continue the good work on other gold fields. John Tong Wai was able to converse easily with Reverend Youngman who was a Eurasian by birth and spoke fluent Chinese. It was not long before the Reverend realised that he had a good prospective trainee catechist to join the ranks of Lue Cheong and others dedicated to converting the heathen to Christianity. He offered to baptise John, followed by a trainee period with his friend Lue Cheong who remained in the Haddon district. However, although John's enthusiasm and dedication to his work was evident, it was soon considered preferable for him to continue his new vocation away from his uncle's disapproval and that of his former workmates from the claim. It was time for a change.

THE MINING OF SOULS

Early in 1885, approximately eighteen months after John's arrival in Victoria, he was baptised by Reverend William Youngman, who was then the Wesleyan minister based in the busy gold mining township of nearby Creswick. John worked as a trainee catechist, but only seven months afterwards he was invited by the committee of the Wesleyan church to undertake extra responsibility from Reverend Youngman to continue his work alone in Creswick as a fully-trained catechist. In March, Reverend Youngman had been notified of his transfer to New South Wales to undertake circuit work for the church. Rising to the challenge, John happily continued for almost two years, working with and preaching the Gospel amongst the mining population of Creswick's Chinatown, situated near the Black Creek Lead and dam. At this stage, the Creswick Chinese were still a visible presence in the township, having earlier numbered at the height of their mining success around 3000 men. Over time they had formed a separate but generally well-tolerated part of the entire Creswick mining community.

However, the responsibility for the welfare of his family back in homeland China had begun to weigh heavily on John's shoulders and by 1887, he became restless because he was aware that his only son was getting older and would soon be growing towards maturity. He was conscious that he had thus far avoided the traditional responsibility expected of him in the home village: his son's future marriage partner had not been arranged and his wife, although receiving a regular stipend from his earnings here, was suffering from his long absence and had not been in good health. She relied on the care and support of his parents and relatives in the village where she remained with their son. It was always considered to be an unacceptable step to contemplate a break with Chinese tradition by removing his family from the homeland and breaking familial ties within the community Soon he would have to make the hard decision about whether to return home and assume the burden of responsibility expected of him, or consider the possibility of asking the Wesleyan Church authorities to finance his passage home with the view to returning with his wife and son. He wished to continue his good work here in the church and as this was his much-preferred option, he eventually applied to the church authorities for permission. To his great disappointment the church authorities refused John the necessary financial means to travel back to China. Disappointed with the decision, John returned to Melbourne where he helped in the Wesleyan Mission for a short period of time. However, feeling quite let down and disillusioned, he decided to leave his position with the Wesleyan Church that had paid him only a miserable stipend and seek some form of work elsewhere.

It was a very troubling and uncertain time for John Tong Wai. He was eventually given word via James Ah Chue, the superintendent missioner at the Presbyterian Mission Church in Ballarat, that a catechist was temporarily required at the gold mining township of Talbot, some distance from Ballarat. He travelled there mostly on foot and spent several months preaching the gospel amongst the Chinese miners in Talbot, but he was soon on the lookout for another position. Once again, John sought help from the Presbyterian Church by accepting an invitation to visit Reverend James Chue in Young Street, Golden Point, meeting with him for the second time. Fortunately for him, James Chue indicated that he was finding the burden of his responsibilities as superintendent over most of the Chinese mining settlements in

Victoria were becoming more than he could manage. Not only did he have the large local Ballarat Chinese population to administer to over several camps, but he was required to travel long distances to other settlements in Victoria such as Geelong, Beechworth, Ararat, Bairnsdale, Warrnambool, Rutherglen, Wahgunyah and Talbot more regularly than he could now manage in the approaching twilight of his mature years. Because John was a much younger man who had impressed him with his energy and intelligence, rare educational ability, and genuine Christian dedication to the work of gaining new souls amongst his countrymen, James Chue considered he was a good choice for an assistant. He offered John the role of resident catechist in the burgeoning gold mining settlement of Little Bendigo, which was on the outskirts of Ballarat near Brown Hill, with a thriving mining community in 1888 of both European and Chinese occupants. By this stage, John had realised that he must defer his hopes and plans for a return to China until he had the means and opportunity to do so. He accepted the position, grateful for the trust that James Chue had placed in him. With great endeavour, he made hasty preparations for the move to the goldfield of Little Bendigo.

Over the ensuing months, the two men became firm friends despite the difference in their ages, aided no doubt by the common goals they shared. Shortly after his arrival, John threw himself into taking charge of Little Bendigo's Chinese community that was situated within a fast developing township. His rented wooden dwelling was very basic, with a couple of front rooms and a lean-to kitchen out back, but adequate for his own simple needs. As far as the eye could see, the surrounding land was covered with prickly gorse bushes that were the unnatural outgrowths of the mined earth which had been disturbed mile upon mile It was completely dug over by the frenzied searchings for alluvial gold of the multitudes of men who had carelessly raped and pillaged the countryside earlier in their frantic hope of reward.

6. Photo of early Nerrina (Little Bendigo)

The hut was situated on land owned by a carpenter, George Stevenson, who had large land holdings in Little Bendigo and lived distantly opposite. He indicated to John that he would be prepared to sell the property to him at a future date if he could meet the payments. The hut was on elevated ground in Lofven Street, within walking distance from the main artery of Humffray Street further downhill, stretching from inner Ballarat East to Brown Hill. It had the appearance of a wasteland, where the soil had been continually disturbed, turned over and discarded. Then it was sprinkled either side of the crude dirt road with small miner's cottages, bordered by the scarred, open-cut mining landmarks of Black Hill in the background, with the forested hills of the Brown Hill range visible traveling further eastwards.

7. Site of old Black Hill Diggings

The municipality of Ballarat East was the working man's side of Ballarat, with few residences to denote wealth or social class and position, in contrast with the separate municipality of Ballarat West. Since the 1860s this burgeoning western township had become the residential heartland of the wealthy, growing middle class and more respectable citizens: some of whom had become upwardly mobile, moving from East to West due to their success at mining investments or in business. But here in Little Bendigo a sprinkling of shops and businesses catered simply to the direct needs of the community. Both the Speedwell and Little Bendigo hotels in the main thoroughfare of Lofven Street were popular meeting places for any social contact or activity amongst the working men of this mining area. The two brick buildings that were visible above the township with elevated rooves, were the St. James Church of England and the Methodist Church across the way that served the spiritual needs of the community, carefully situated on high ground and well removed from the taint and turmoil of mining below.

The Chinese Mission Hall was a simple, crude wooden building near the creek that crossed over a little further up Lofven Street and was surrounded by Chinese market gardens situated on the fertile and swampy river flats. John Tong Wai had a short uphill walk along Lofven Street from his dwelling to the wooden Mission building where he would conduct his services and attend to the pastoral care of his new flock. By this stage, some had already abandoned mining and turned to the more predictable earnings from their vegetable gardens. He soon got to know Fancy John, who had his vegetable garden well situated between the creek and the Mission Hall and who was one of the first Chinese to greet John when he arrived. He was a regular face in the local area, seen walking with his ta'am loaded up with produce from his garden and regularly hawking his vegetables to various households about the district. 'You likee flesh vegetables?' you could hear him say, with a wide smile spread across his good-natured face. He still wore his traditional wide-brimmed straw hat and loose clothing, plus sandaled feet and he had retained the long, braided queue which hung down his back.

Those Chinese miners who still relied on working and reworking the soil for the elusive gold deposits around the Woah Hawp Dam were concentrated in this area, pitted with shallow mine shafts and with access to the water so necessary for processing the fine specks of alluvial gold. No longer were the rich pickings of golden nuggets being found in the paydirt, and from the tremendous toil required, few men could claim much more than a meagre return for their efforts. The Chinese-owned Woah Hawp Hong Kong mine and the Monte Christo quartz mine employed those men who worked for wages deep underground, but it was said that many Chinese were superstitious about working at great depths, as they believed that devils lurked deep underground in the corners and most Chinese were happier to work near the surface. This meant that they were often content to rework the abandoned ground of old diggings. Any money that could be spared was sent home to their villages in China to repay their debts and support the families these men had left behind. Sadly, some of them had been living and working this solitary existence for so many years that their hopes of making enough money to pay their passages and return home were fast diminishing with each passing year.

John quickly made his way around the Chinese community to make himself known and offer them any personal or spiritual assistance he could. Most of these men were from the Sze Yap district in Kwangtung province and they had been poor, illiterate farmers who could neither read nor write for themselves. In return for rendering his assistance with any written matters, John invited them to attend his services and learn about the teachings of the Gospel. Because he was educated in China and had held a schoolteacher position back home, he had no difficulty in winning the respect and support of his new flock on Sundays when he requested their attendance. Besides an extra Sunday service, he also conducted weekly Bible classes and prayer meetings, so he was proud to report to James Chue and also in his written annual report to the Presbyterian authorities that his attendance numbers had risen dramatically since his arrival at Little Bendigo. He enjoyed his work with the people and his only regret stemmed from loneliness and the thoughts of his father, Liu Chou Hock, and mother, Shin Nue. He was also troubled by thoughts of his wife and the young son he had never been a father to since leaving the homeland so many years ago. He kept in regular, close contact with James Chue, whom he now regarded as a close friend and confidant. James was to be ordained as a fully-fledged missionary of the Presbyterian Church later in 1891 and he invited John to attend the ceremony at St. Andrews Kirk in Ballarat, the imposing bluestone Presbyterian cathedral where this special occasion took place.

8. St Andrews Kirk (recent)

John had undertaken some of the extra workload from Reverend Chue since he took on his Little Bendigo responsibilities, with regular visits to the Benevolent Asylum. Here there were some destitute Chinese who had succumbed to opium addiction with resultant poverty, and they were dependent on the charity of the churches. Quite often he intervened on behalf of fellow Chinese who were assaulted and even robbed, by reporting these incidents to the Ballarat Police, but the offenders were never caught. Sometimes he was also required to represent them in court, due to their language difficulties. Suicide was another problem he had to contend with such as the case of Ack Gow in 1894, an ailing miner aged 70 years. The suicide was reported to the police by John Tong Wai and later recorded in the *Ballarat Star* newspaper. He had committed suicide by drowning himself in a dam at Nerrina (Little Bendigo). John Tong Wai was visiting him and had arranged for him to be collected and removed to hospital, but the deceased had objected, saying that he would rather die than go there. His body was found face down in the dam a short distance from his hut when the cab arrived to collect him. On another occasion, after 9 weeks of regular visits to see Lee Cheok, an ailing elderly miner who was suffering from bad asthma and had previously refused hospital, John found him dead in his hut. These occurrences happened to elderly miners with sad regularity. He also undertook distant visits to the other Mission stations that were under James Chue's care, often walking long distances as the only option when transport was unavailable; this was often as far as Geelong, Ararat and Talbot. Surprisingly, on a couple of occasions he was reported in the newspapers as traveling interstate. He travelled to Western Australia in 1902, and in 1910 to Broken Hill, New South Wales as a temporary replacement to take charge of the Chinese Missions there. It was left to Mary Tong Wai to carry on with the family responsibilities until his return. He was strong and spare in build and enjoyed the physical challenges, for which he was to become well known as a good walker.

It was with pride that his reports to the Presbyterian Church authorities enumerated the numbers of Chinese who regularly attended his services, but ironically, the actual number of converts to Christianity were pathetically few. The Little Bendigo Chinese were loyal supporters of John and generous with their financial contributions to his Mission, but reluctant to renounce their old ways and beliefs. Many were still visiting the Joss house situated off Main Road near Golden Point whenever the opportunity presented itself. Heroically, John laboured on in the following years, with his loneliness and failure because of poor wages, to save enough money so that someday soon he would be able to secure a passage back to China; he was longing to fulfil his dream to return with his wife and child. Even though he was aware that there were some mixed marriages between male Chinese and local Ballarat women, John was not prepared to ignore his filial responsibilities back home, added to the fact that he would commit bigamy against the teachings of the church if he was to seek another wife. Although the church authorities considered it preferable for a catechist to have a wife, he was also aware that it was frowned upon by the church to have a racially mixed marriage. Therefore, he knew it would be safer and more preferable to have a wife of his own kind. Racial prejudice was always hovering beneath the surface and John was aware that it resurfaced easily when economic pressures were greatest. The people of Golden Point who lived amongst and in close proximity to the Chinese were not such a problem, but it was easy to stir hostility amongst those who had little direct or personal contact with his fellow countrymen. Superstitions and gossip prevailed at the lack of Chinese women amongst them, and he was convinced that fetching his Chinese wife was the only option he could consider. The question was, how he was going to achieve this without the necessary means to do so in the future? He busied himself in the ensuing years after his arrival at Little Bendigo and from the pittance the church paid him, he continued to send regular money back home to his family in the village to ensure that they would be cared for. As time marched on, his heart was heavy with worry, and he also carried the burden of guilt for the long years of their separation.

Towards November in 1890, after nearly three years dedicated to his Little Bendigo flock, John paid a visit to see his friend Reverend Chue to discuss his concerns. James Chue was sympathetic and informed John that because of his devoted and faithful service to the Little Bendigo Chinese and the success of his work over these past years, he was making a recommendation to the Presbyterian Church to grant him six months paid leave of absence. He advised John that he would request the church to finance his return to China in the following year for the purpose of further missionary training, followed by his subsequent return to Australia with his wife and child. At hearing this news from his old friend, John was overjoyed and dared to be hopeful that this time he may have earned a favourable response to his personal need. It was only weeks later before James Chue was able to inform him, with a huge smile on his face, that the decision was favourable, and he was to make the arrangements for his passage home. The date was to be decided at James's convenience, given that the extra duties of care for Little Bendigo would fall on his own shoulders whilst John was away on leave. Matters moved quickly from that moment and in May 1891, John set sail from Melbourne on the *Airlie* bound for Hong Kong with high hopes of reuniting with his family at last.

State Library of Queensland
John Oxley Library

The "Airlie" (2,337 gross tons), built in 1884 was sold in 1904 to Burns Philp and Company. She was broken up in China in 1911

9. Ship "Airlie" photo

The sea voyage was uneventful, but tragedy intervened in a way that John had not foreseen. Upon his arrival at the village of Wang Tung,

John was met by the sad faces of family members who informed him that he was too late. His wife had been in failing health for a long time and she had taken a turn for the worse a month before his arrival. It was her dying wish that their son should go with him if he intended to leave the village again and return to Tsin Chin Shan (New Gold Mountain).

PARENTAL DECISION

John Tong Wai was faced with a dilemma! If he returned to Australia with Jo Lau Lung, the eleven-year-old son he had now re-named Joseph Thomas, he would be hampered in his work at Little Bendigo. The boy did not know any language but his own, he was illiterate, and he was totally ignorant of any other culture than his own familiar village life in Wang Tung. John thought it would be unfair to his son to leave him alone in Little Bendigo for the long periods necessitated by his pastoral work; neither would it be adequate to leave him in the care of strangers who spoke an alien language and had no understanding of Chinese practices and customs. John came to the conclusion that the only solution would be if he could find a new wife before he left China and returned to Australia in several months' time. Due to the strong cultural practices and beliefs upheld by Chinese Government policy which dictated against Chinese women leaving their village life in the homeland – particularly young, unwedded females – he decided that the only choice he had was to approach an orphanage. Many female babies were discarded at birth, due to the poverty of peasant Chinese who prioritised the value of male babies when there were too many mouths to feed. He had heard that the Lutheran Mission ran the large Bethesda Orphanage for rescued female babies in Hong Kong, where orphaned girls received a rudimentary education with some training in domestic skills.

10. Bethesda Lutheran Orphanage photo

Whilst in Hong Kong, he arranged a visit to discuss his problem with the missionary in charge who turned out to be a German woman. He explained that he was hoping to explore the prospect of selecting a future wife; a young female they deemed as suitable to take back with him to Australia. Due to the length of his stay, which included further studies he had agreed to undertake for the church at the University of Canton, he was able to visit the orphanage on several occasions. He was finally informed of their prospective choice and permitted to meet her. He was introduced to a small, slender, and very shy young Chinese woman named Mary Song who was eighteen years old and came originally from one of the Sze Yap clans; her parentage was unknown because she had been one of the many female babies abandoned outside the orphanage or found discarded elsewhere and finally left to the mercies of the Mission staff. The religious order was comprised of German women and these young, unmarried Chinese females were placed under their protection, for the purpose of their basic education and religious conversion. The head missioner told John that Mary was a gentle and dutiful girl who was a God-fearing Christian. She said she had much faith in Mary who would become a good wife and mother to eleven-year-old Joseph if John was prepared to marry her and give her a good life. Understandably, young Mary was hesitant and nervous when they first met, but despite the difference of more than a ten-year age gap between them, John was impressed with the fact that she appeared to be intelligent and greeted him with a few stilted words of the English language that she had been taught by her carers. All sang her praises as being capable domestically and an experienced cook who would make a good potential stepmother. Furthermore, John had also presented favourably as a respectable prospect, because, by Chinese standards, he was well educated and still a tall, good-looking man for his age.

Ultimately, John felt that he had found the best solution for young Joseph and also for himself. He considered that, with God's help, he would devote himself to his new family, knowing his life and work at Little Bendigo would be much better with a Chinese wife and son. He would no longer be plagued by loneliness and the temptations of an inappropriate marriage with a woman of European descent, less acceptable to the Church and gold mining community he wished to dedicate his life's work to. He informed the orphanage of his decision and made the necessary arrangements to undergo a legal marriage ceremony. He booked passages for himself, Mary and young Joseph on the ship *Guthrie* on 28th November 1891, where they would soon embark from Hong Kong for the long sea voyage to the Port of Melbourne. John could only afford to pay for steerage, which meant that it was going to be an arduous trip, with no comforts and on the lower decks where sea sickness was at its worst. Poor Mary must have been under a great deal of strain when embarking from Hong Kong aboard ship: firstly because she was responsible for the care of her new stepson, Joseph, who may also have been ill equipped for such a journey, and, secondly, she was also a stranger to her husband. Apart from the fear and discomfort she experienced, she endured extreme loneliness and lack of companionship due to the absence of any other Chinese females in a total of twelve adult passengers. Also, she was unable to converse with these other passengers, due to language difficulties. There was an absence of Chinese on board because, more recently, the dwindling returns from alluvial gold mining meant that the numbers of Chinese gold seekers now traveling to Australia had declined dramatically. By far the greater numbers of single men were now making the return voyage to China if they could possibly pay their passage back home. Therefore, Mary found that she was isolated with only young Joseph and her husband John for company. Despite the travails of the journey, the days passed into weeks without any major mishaps, and it was with great relief that they finally viewed the land silhouetted against the skyline and passed through the heads, bound for the Port of Melbourne where they were soon to disembark with their meagre belongings. It was the beginning of a totally new and alien life for Mary and the boy, but also quite a challenging prospect for John Tong Wai, with a strange new wife and son to settle in and adjust to his own pattern of life and work in this promising land: the land which, in his eyes, begged his return to Little Bendigo.

They were able to purchase tickets for a train ride from Melbourne to Ballarat, and the journey undertaken was a long, exhausting one, given their earlier travails of embarkation from the ship and finding their way with their luggage to the Spencer Street station. They were too tired to take any notice of the curious stares from other passengers on the journey. When they finally arrived at Ballarat, John decided it would be best to take Mary and the boy to meet Reverend James Chue at the manse in Young Street. Although it was not such a long walk along Main Road and uphill through the Chinese village at Golden Point, they struggled to carry their belongings between them. Glad to arrive, they were greeted warmly by James Chue who ushered them into the front room where he had made preparations for them to have a meal with him. It was followed by a buggy ride with James Chue at the reins, taking them along Humffray Street and on to their wooden dwelling in Lofven Street where they would be settled permanently. Fortunately, James Chue had arranged for the interior of the hut to be cleaned and all was in readiness for them to move in and rest their tired, travel-weary bodies for the night. He took his farewell of them with a kindly wave and set off again on the return trip to the manse at Golden Point before the onset of nightfall. All was so strange to Mary and the boy, but they were now too tired to take much notice, other than to fall into the crude wooden bunks that awaited them. Tomorrow was to be another day for all that was strange and new to challenge them.

Early next morning, just after daybreak, John had risen and he had the fire burning in the fireplace already, with the kettle on to heat some water for their needs. He knew that everything was going to be strange to his newly acquired wife and child, so he was prepared to patiently teach and support them with each new challenge until they became accustomed to daily life in their new environs of Little Bendigo. Their first visitor for the day was Fancy John, who was standing by the front door in traditional Chinese garb, with his long queue and large straw hat, carrying a basket brimming over with vegetables he had freshly picked that morning from his plentiful garden. He politely greeted John Tong Wai and, with hands clenched together, he bowed repeatedly when introduced to Mary and young Joseph.

Fortunately for them both, Fancy John had come from the Sze Yap district in the Kwangtung Province, so they were able to speak to each other in familiar Cantonese dialect. Mary was extremely shy and reserved because she was so fearfully overwhelmed by all the challenges she faced at this stage. Hesitantly, however, she warmed to the hospitality and familiar greeting they received from Fancy John; he was to be a close neighbour and regular contact Mary would learn to rely on in the days to come. Other than a few market gardeners like Fancy John situated on the rich soil of the flood plain by the creek, there were only non- Chinese residents living in Lofven Street, but the Tong Wai family's location was quite isolated as they had no directly adjoining neighbouring properties. This made it difficult for Mary and Joseph to meet many other residents in the street, also complicated because of the language barrier which divided them and made it impossible to speak with the Europeans.

The question then arose about the best solution to be found for John's eleven-year-old son, Joseph. John decided the best school for young Joseph to attend was the Brown Hill State School, quite a long, lonely walk downhill from Lofven Street and along Humffray Street.

11. Brown Hill State School

However, he found that Joseph was reluctant to attend, thinking of the language barrier he faced and his unfamiliarity with what difficulties lay ahead of him. He soon found that his apprehension was justified. The fact that he still kept his long hair in the traditional queue of his homeland and wore his customary strange, loose clothing became an instant source of alienation and ridicule that he found hard to bear. In the school yard, from the very first day, he was laughed at and taunted with cruel remarks, especially by the boys; he found it impossible to understand any of the requirements expected of him in the classroom where he sat, isolated, traumatised and uncomprehending. The headmaster was unsure of what he could do with the boy, but he had assured Reverend Tong Wai that he would do his best to include him if he continued to attend daily and persevere with learning how to speak the English language. However, it was not long before Joseph silently refused to go to the school and would secretly return to Mary as soon as his father disappeared from the hut for the day. His feelings of alienation continued and whenever Joseph was on his own, he found himself the object of laughter, scorn and abuse by the other boys his age, who enjoyed recognising the torment the boy was going through. Finally, he confessed to his father that he refused to go any more and, by this stage, John was forced to accept the situation and allow him to stay home with Mary, who understood and was sympathetic towards his feelings.

Only six months after his arrival in Little Bendigo, Joseph was going on a message to the Little Bendigo store for his stepmother, Mary, when he was confronted by a group of three boys of a similar age, who were blocking his path. At first, he was ridiculed with the usual words of 'Chow' and 'Chink' and sworn at. Then, as he nervously passed by, one of the boys picked up a large quartz rock and threw it at his head, cutting it above the eye quite badly. He almost fell down, due to the heaviness of the blow and staggered towards the store as the boys ran off. As he entered the building, the storekeeper was shocked to see the blood pouring down Joseph's face and he hastened to send a message for Dr Hardy because he could see it was necessary to get medical treatment from the doctor to treat the wound. When the doctor arrived, he cleaned the wound and proceeded to stitch the large gash and apply a bandage. The storekeeper felt sorry for poor young Joseph, saying, 'You cannot walk home in that state, my boy. Just wait while I hook up the horse and cart and I will take you back.' He kindly delivered Joseph home without any further mishaps. Mary was quite distressed when she saw the bandaged head and the terrible state Joseph was in when he arrived. The matter was reported to the local Ballarat Police by an angry John Tong Wai when he returned home and it was taken up and later dealt with in court, with Joseph testifying via an interpreter. Doctor Hardy also testified as a witness to verify the fact that he had treated the head wound that had resulted from the stone throwing incident. As reported in the *Ballarat Star* the boy named Edward Brain who actually threw the stone was sentenced to a month's imprisonment, with the surety of £10 to be paid by the boy's mother for a suspension of the sentence and a twelve-month behaviour bond. This was only one of several such incidents involving poor Joseph. On another occasion it was reported in the local newspaper that a boy called John Sherry was also charged for abusing Joseph in Humffray Street and attempting to throw a stone at him. He was duly charged a fine of twenty shillings, or in default of payment, a month in gaol. It was due to the respect that John Tong Wai had earnt from the community for his good work with the Chinese mission that, un-customarily, he gained a measure of justice for his son. Many of the other Chinese were unsuccessful and those who attended court expressed their concern about the problem of stone throwing as a too-frequent occurrence that resulted from the unwarranted hostility and prejudice directed against them. Ultimately, John relented to Joseph's pleas following this incident. Reluctantly, he decided that Joseph should continue to remain at home with his stepmother, Mary, during the many long days whilst he was away attending to his duties and not at home in the district himself. He recognised that, without any education, Joseph would be at a great disadvantage, but he decided he would endeavour to try and teach the boy some rudimentary language whenever he could. However, this situation inevitably condemned Joseph to the same solitary existence that his stepmother was to experience. He would have no further contact with boys his own age, but he was able to do chores for Fancy John and assist with some of the manual labour for the Chinese market gardeners up nearer to the creek. He was happier and more familiar with this type of work, which he had undergone back home in the family village of Wang Tung.

John was keen for his wife, Mary, to be baptised in the beautiful Presbyterian interior of St Andrew's Kirk in Sturt Street, Ballarat, where he hoped that he would eventually be ordained as a minister of the church himself, so he made arrangements for Mary to attend soon after they were settled and she had regained a little more confidence to undergo the ceremony. It was noted in the *Ballarat Star* that the event took place on the Sabbath day of 24th January 1892, with Mary and five Chinese men being baptised in the presence of a large congregation. It must have been an overwhelming experience for young Mary at this time, when she had only been in the country since the previous November and she still had only a rudimentary grasp of this new language. Much later, in 1905, John's ordination as a minister of the Presbyterian Church was conducted at this same venue, with a large attendance of official church representatives. For John, it was a proud moment and an important milestone of achievement in his adopted country. His status had been elevated from Missionary to Minister and in the eyes of both the church and the local community he had earned his place as the Reverend Tong Wai.

Following her baptism, it was not long before Mary discovered that she was expecting her first child. As the months went by and the birth would soon be imminent, she became very apprehensive about being so isolated and she worried that, when her time came, her husband would be unavailable to support her in her time of need.

Further along in Lofven Street, a Mrs Stevens was known to the local community as a capable woman who occasionally acted as a midwife and who could be sent for by young Joseph when Mary was sure that her labour had begun. At the request of John Tong Wai, Mrs Stevens assured him that she would make herself available to help with the birth. 'Now don't you worry, Reverend, I have delivered many babies and I will make sure she is looked after when the time comes,' she had said reassuringly. John was increasingly called upon to relieve his friend Reverend Chue with the long-distance visits he was obliged to make regularly in support of his 'flock' at other locations in Victoria. This often necessitated those long walks on foot between available transport such as the train or horse-drawn vehicles. Consequently, the days were often long, and Mary was required to spend a lot of time on her own with only Joseph for company during John's many absences. Her grasp of English was still very limited, and she was forced to rely on young Joseph for any regular conversation she had with him in her own Cantonese language. They both experienced a sense of continual isolation and cultural alienation in this strange, foreign land in which they were captive.

It was in November 1892, almost twelve months since her arrival in Ballarat, that nineteen-year-old Mary realised that the birth of her first child was imminent. It was verging summer and the hot weather was becoming quite difficult to endure in the confines of their wooden dwelling. It was cramped and airless during the high temperatures they were experiencing during the day. On 15th November it was one of those days when John had set off early that morning for one of his extended visits to a distant mining settlement of Chinese occupants who were his customary responsibility to oversee and convert to Christianity wherever possible. He informed Mary that he would not be returning until late evening that day and advised her to send Joseph for any help she may require from Mrs Stevens; she was a short distance further on in Lofven Street and her husband, George, a carpenter by trade, presently owned the property they lived in.

By mid-morning, it was obvious to young Mary that she was having labour pains, which were increasing in their regularity and intensity. She was stricken with fear and filled with apprehension and dread at the situation she was in. Joseph was hovering helplessly by in the adjoining room, with alarm written all over his features. When her waters broke, she cried out to him for help and begged him to run for Mrs Stevens and bring her back with him. He burst out of the front door and ran bare footed up the road in a panic of sudden action. Banging on the door, he repeatedly called out in his limited English, 'Help! You come. Help baby!' He continued to bang his fists on the door until it opened to reveal Mrs Stevens standing wide-hipped in her large apron, with her hands squarely placed on either side. 'Alright, boy, don't fret yourself. I'm a-comin' as soon as I get my basket an' shawl.' She shook her head, saying to herself, 'The poor wee lass, she must be frightened down there with nobody to comfort her and no family at all.'

When she entered the room, she saw Mary stretched out on the crude wooden bed, with her knees up and perspiration trickling down her face, whimpering in a picture of distress and fear. 'Help,' she managed to say in broken sobs. 'I afraid this baby!'. Mrs Stevens said, 'There, dearie, I will try to make you more comfortable,' and she proceeded to sponge Mary's face with a wet cloth and examine the stage of her labour to gain some idea of how the birth was progressing. Meanwhile, young Joseph remained well out of sight and blocked his ears to the sounds of Mary's distressed and painful cries which echoed continually throughout the day. As the afternoon progressed, Mrs Stevens became increasingly worried, because the contractions continued, but Mary was visibly exhausted and growing weaker by the hour. In desperation, she sent young Joseph with a written message to the General storekeeper further up Lofven Street, asking him to send for the doctor urgently, as she thought Mary was in trouble and unable to deliver the baby normally. For such a small person, this baby appeared to be extremely large and difficult to deliver, with many hours now passing.

Joseph was pale faced as he returned, repeating the same words over and over again, 'Doctor soon, doctor he soon.' However, it was many agonising hours later that the doctor finally arrived in his cart, carrying his leather bag and hurrying into the room where Mary now lay unconscious and in a grave state, her face streaked with perspiration and etched with the prolonged rigors of her unendurable pain. At this late stage, fourteen hours had passed without the attendance of the doctor, and Mrs Stevens felt desperately worried, realising that the life of the baby and the mother were both critically endangered. Despite the best efforts of Mrs Stevens to assist that day, she realised that Mary was losing the battle. Poor young Joseph had been forced to stand witness to the agony of Mary's screams echoing continuously into the afternoon. It seemed to him that after fourteen hours of agonising labour she had mercifully lost consciousness and had no more pain, but unfortunately, by then she had begun to haemorrhage. Tragically, the doctor had ignored the urgency of the message and it was too late! It was with weary resignation and almost an air of inevitability that when the doctor finally arrived, it was only to sign the death certificate. In a matter-of-fact tone of voice, he announced to Mrs Stevens, 'We have lost her and the baby also.'

Due to the rigors and length of the birth and the last-minute arrival of the doctor, the baby had been delivered stillborn. As a matter of routine, he signed the necessary death certificate and took his leave, requesting that Mrs Stevens be the bearer of such tragic news when John Tong Wai finally returned from his travels later that night. Until such time, she waited in trepidation for John's arrival; she felt obliged to remain with the completely distraught boy, who was overcome with the loss of his young stepmother: she who had been his only companion in this harsh, alien and uncompromising environment that they had been thrust into so recently. The death certificate recorded the barest facts of the event, but the human elements involved with this tragedy almost surpassed the imagination. Young Joseph was severely traumatised by the event and plagued with unrealistic feelings of guilt from the burden of responsibility he felt at this tragic outcome. He vowed he would never forget the sounds which rang in his ears incessantly throughout that terrible day. It haunted his memory of these events that he vividly recalled in later life until the day he died at the age of 74 years.

When John returned, travel sore and weary that night, he was confronted with the terrible news of that day's events which Mrs Stevens related in between her tears. It may have seemed to her that John Tong Wai took the news with more stoicism and acceptance than was customary for such tragic circumstances, but John was sustained by his strong faith and his implicit trust that it was 'God's will', and he must find a way to accept it. By nature, he had a strong reserve and an instinctive desire for privacy. He was not accustomed to displaying his innermost feelings before strangers. For days that lasted into weeks there were persistent rumours passed around the township, hinting at the possibility of negligence in the absence of care given to young Mary in her desperate hour of need during and before the birth. It was covertly reported in the death notices as a 'short illness', and the *Ballarat Star* reported the local gossip as unpleasant rumours, seeking to quell the spreading of such talk. Despite a letter of complaint that was circulated among members of the community, little eventuated. The letter was sent to the Ballarat Police within two weeks of the tragedy regarding these rumours of negligence, requesting an investigation into the situation; however, the police claimed that there was no evidence produced to support such gossip. The question remained in the minds of many who had known her, especially the Chinese who had themselves known injustice and experienced much prejudice and lack of care. Although young Mary had been in the colony for barely twelve months and she had lived quietly and unobtrusively as the only Chinese female in the district, the newspaper reported that she had been 'much esteemed by the Chinese and European residents.' These remarks were echoed in sympathy by many who heard about the tragedy which had befallen Reverend Tong Wai and his recently arrived family. Young Joseph was heartbroken and feeling completely bereft without his kind stepmother and only companion during the long days they had shared together since their arrival.

Mary's funeral service was conducted before a local gathering in the Little Bendigo Mission Church. In a show of support for this sorrowful event there followed a large, solemn procession of mourners, both Chinese and European, who walked behind the horse-drawn hearse the distance along Humffray Street, turning behind the railway line up Scott's Parade, across Lydiard Street and along Doveton Street to the new cemetery on the north side of Ballarat. Four of the coffin bearers were fellow Chinese and many among the pall bearers were also Chinese, including John's friend Reverend James Chue who was one of the officiating ministers. At just nineteen years of age, young Mary Song was gently lowered into the soil of her freshly dug grave, placed to rest permanently in the land where she had been a forlorn stranger for the past twelve months of her short life. Her unnamed, stillborn child was placed in the grave beside her; their existence soon to be largely forgotten, with the tragic event too painful to ever pass the lips of John Tong Wai for the remainder of his days. Sadly, this silence resulted in subsequent generations never realising or mentioning that a second wife had ever existed. Thus it was a complete shock when I made my initial search at the Ballarat cemetery that revealed the existence of an earlier Tong Way grave: one that testified to the tragic death and burial of young Mary Song, the forgotten second wife. Her short and tragic sojourn in Ballarat was registered, along with the later deaths of Albert, Stephen and Gladys, the young children subsequently born to his third wife, Mary Kong. Apart from the earlier private recollections of Joseph, it seemed as if a second wife had never even lived, in terms of how this event had not registered in the Tong Way family memories of the current generation.

Thus, it was that poor young Joseph, who suffered the loss of his young stepmother most keenly at the time, was left to grieve alone, due to the long absences of his father who doggedly carried on with his responsibilities, regardless of his personal loss. Fancy John was the only friend that 'Joe' was able to spend regular time with and unburden the heavy weight of his sadness and sense of isolation to. As he grew older, he assisted Fancy John more with the market garden and accompanied him when he carried his vegetable produce in the wooden pushcart to hawk around the neighbourhood. Fancy John would often give him a few hard-earned coins for his labours whenever he could spare a little from his own meagre earnings. In his untimely loss, John Tong Wai was sustained by the increasing demands of his work 'bringing the Gospel to the heathen' at Little Bendigo, and the friendship and respect of Reverend James Chue. However, as time passed by, John was still plagued by the difficulties of his situation, with Joseph to care for and no wife to share the domestic responsibilities of his life's work or to lighten the load he presently carried. He was still conscious of the added difficulties he faced if he married a woman 'not of his own kind' in the eyes of the church, so he unburdened his concerns and worries to his friend James Chue when he called at the manse in Young Street for their customary regular meeting. Of course, James was sympathetic and well-aware of John's situation. John had exhausted the good will and financial assistance that had been forthcoming from the church in this matter, so the possibility of returning to China in the hope of finding another Chinese woman to marry was negligible indeed.

However, the germ of an idea had formulated in James Chue's mind, and he outlined the idea to John in the hope that a solution may be found. He had recently decided to apply for leave from his long years of service to the Presbyterian Church in Australia, because he wished to make a trip to visit his homeland where, like a typical Chinese immigrant, he hoped that one day he would make it his final, permanent resting place. He planned to ask John if he would undertake the extra duties and responsibilities of the Golden Point Mission during his absence on the understanding that John would agree to do this, plus tend to his own congregation at Little Bendigo whilst he was away. In return, he thought he may also be able to help John by arranging the choice of a third Chinese wife on his behalf whilst he was visiting in China. This was the only way John would succeed in gaining a suitable wife, as the church would not be persuaded to finance another trip for many future years. Because John felt so strongly against making a mixed marriage, he was happy to accept James' offer and so he provided him with the details and whereabouts of the same Bethesda Lutheran orphanage in Hong Kong where he had first chosen Mary Song, his late second wife such a very short time ago.

All arrangements were made for his departure and shortly afterwards, in February 1893, James Chue set sail for China, with great anticipation to see his homeland once again after so many years in Australia. Upon his arrival in Hong Kong, true to his word, he soon made contact with the Bethesda Orphanage and arranged a meeting to explain the tragic loss of young Mary in childbirth and John's pressing need to re-marry a woman from his own country of birth once more. Of course, this time it was to be not of John's choosing, but with total reliance upon his trusted friend James and the same Lutheran woman in charge that he had completely depended upon before. James explained to her that young Mary had been a most satisfactory, devoted wife to John and that she had treated young Joseph, her stepson, with kindness during their brief life together in Australia before the tragedy of her difficult confinement and death.

By the time James Chue had satisfied her about the details of his request, she carefully selected another young, slightly older woman of twenty years as suitable to undertake the journey and the daunting responsibility she would be faced with as did Mary, her younger predecessor. She would also experience this alien new country and culture, with an entirely unknown husband and adolescent son to care for. Nevertheless, it was considered that this young woman had enough strength of character and Christian faith to recommend her and furthermore, she did have the valuable asset of an education provided by the nuns, speaking a few words of English, and she was able to read and write fluently in her own tongue of Cantonese. Her birth name was A Kie Maiey Kong and she was the daughter of a poor peasant couple, Snig Kong and Ah Non from Hong Kong who could not afford to raise a female child. Hence, she had been placed into the care of the orphanage as an infant. Her traditionally bound feet were greatly disapproved of by the orphanage and subsequently the process was discontinued, and the bindings removed immediately to avoid any further damage. Strangely, she was also given the same name of Mary. The marriage was arranged legally by proxy and Mary undertook the journey in the ship named the *Airlie*, chaperoned by James Chue and traveling in steerage class.

Fortunately for her, she had the company of another Chinese female named Jessie Jo Leong who had also been married by proxy and was traveling to meet her new husband, a miner named Peter Quong whose clan name was also Liu; he had come from the same village as John Tong Wai and was now living nearby on the same Ballarat goldfield.

When they embarked for the long sea journey to this unknown land of Tsin Chin Shan, both Mary and Jessie found great comfort in each other's company and their similar situations, so that a friendship developed between them. It was a friendship that was to sustain them in their loneliness and the everyday challenges of family life in this country for many years to come.

Thus, in the company of James Chue, they arrived on board the *Airlie* to disembark in Melbourne on 13th October 1893. Upon their arrival, these two young Chinese women created great curiosity amongst the many observers, dressed in their exotic, traditional garments. It was such an unusual scene to witness their meeting for the very first time with their pre-arranged husbands; consequently, it was reported in the press as a newsworthy event, describing how these two Chinese women were to be finally introduced in person to these total strangers and their future husbands with whom they would share this new life in Australia. On the voyage Mary had brought with her a beautiful Chinese costume which she had hoped to wear as her wedding outfit in the anticipated marriage ceremony, but James Chue strongly advised against it as it was deemed by the church of John Tong Wai as unsuitable for a Christian ceremony at the time. Both Mary and Jessie felt quite upset that their traditional clothing was rejected, but they obeyed, recognising that they had little option but to comply.

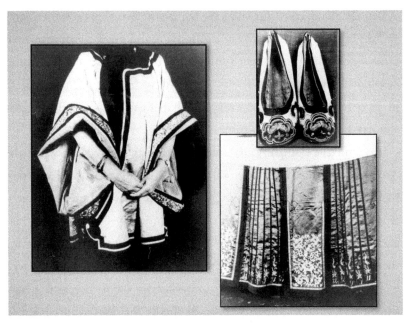

12. Mary's Chinese wedding outfit

Mary had also brought with her the tiny silk shoes which had been made to fit her deformed feet that had been tightly bound before she was abandoned as a child at the Bethesda Orphanage. Although the orphanage had removed the original bindings, the toes had been forcibly bent back beneath the foot and the arch had also been broken. Consequently, much damage had been done to affect her ability to walk normally. For the rest of her life she was restricted to a shuffle, not able to walk long distances, and most of the time she wore soft Chinese slippers on her feet. It was decided that there would be a double Christian wedding of the two couples, considering that both brides had arrived in Ballarat together, so the wedding took place at number 6 Young Street in Golden Point where the Chinese manse and Presbyterian Mission Church were. The women were expected to wear the conventional Victorian-style fashions which befitted the social norms of Ballarat culture and society. Thus, the formal wedding portrait displays the diminutive forms of the two young women standing with their smooth, softly rounded faces expressionless beside their husbands, their hair parted and drawn back in severe Victorian buns, wearing similar severely styled gowns of the period. One wonders at the thoughts which must have been passing through their minds at the strangeness of this occasion.

13 Tong Wai and Quong - double wedding

After the ceremony, Peter and Jessie Jo Quong were to reside in the Mount Pleasant locality of Ballarat, not far from the church in Young Street, and the Tong Wais returned to the crude wooden hut in Little Bendigo, where John Tong Wai resumed his normal pastoral duties and introduced Joseph, now almost an adult at thirteen years of age, to his third mother and second stepmother. It was a challenging beginning for Mary, but she was a practical personality and she set about trying to make their humble wooden dwelling as much like a home as she was able. She was happy to remain at home most of the time, without venturing far in Lofven Street, due to their isolation from other neighbours and also her inability to walk far. John had begun to grow a small vegetable patch and herb garden and he liked to undertake the cooking of the evening meals when he was at home. Mary was unaccustomed to cooking Chinese food due to her upbringing in the orphanage. John also purchased most of the household supplies, so it was unnecessary for Mary to shop or venture far from home. She did manage to keep in contact with her friend Jessie Jo Quong and see her occasionally. It was on these occasions that they were happy to converse in their own language and exchange their strange and often challenging experiences of life in Ballarat.

14. Photo of Quong family

It was not long before they each found that motherhood was on the horizon. Mary Tong Wai gave birth to her firstborn son, baptised Saml Lui without any complications on 25th August 1894, much to the joy and relief of his thankful parents. Two years later, they were blessed with another son, Hedley David, my grandfather in June 1896, followed by a daughter, Doris, born on 5th April 1898. Sadly, the third son, Humffray, born in April 1900, died after only eight days, from the effects of a premature birth. The remaining three children spent their early childhood in the wooden dwelling at Lofven Street in Little Bendigo, largely isolated from the rest of the community, both European and Chinese. There was little respite for Mary who was content to remain at home tending to the children, with only the occasional contact with her friend Jessie; they were both raising families, and distance was a barrier for them both to contend with. Mary also discovered that her husband's position elevated him somewhat in the eyes of both the European and Asian communities and this necessitated the family maintaining a certain social reserve, especially with the all-male, mainly working class, uneducated Chinese in the district. Gordon was the fourth son, born on 22nd February 1901. Unfortunately, from an early age he suffered from epileptic fits following an accident when a gate fell on his head: this affected his development which created an extra burden for Mary and took up much of her time and energy caring for him.

When Saml, the eldest son, reached school age, instead of being enrolled further uphill at the Little Bendigo State school where attendances were falling rapidly due to the poor returns from gold yields, he attended the Brown Hill State School downhill in Thompson Street: the same school his half-brother, Joseph, had experienced so briefly before-hand. He found that he was still the only Chinese student in the entire school. However, he was not deterred from this circumstance as his half-brother, Joseph, had been. He was born here and determined to make the most of his opportunities, with the particular encouragement of his father. He demonstrated a singlemindedness and an eagerness to learn right from the outset. Every day he had a long, solitary walk along the rough, uneven dirt road from Lofven Street. He went down the steep slope via Stawell Street, past Taylor's Brickworks in the gully on the left, then around the corner, turning left by the Dew Drop Inn on the right-hand corner and into Humffray Street. It was quite a distance for a six-year-old. Fortunately, the school grounds were no longer pitted with disused mine shafts as in earlier years: they were subsequently filled in due to the tragic drowning of a five-year old boy, George Avert, who fell in and drowned before he could be rescued in time. The school was a substantial brick building in 1900, with several classrooms that catered up to the eighth grade. Saml was encouraged by his father to work hard and value the opportunity that education would provide him with in the future, as it had for John Tong Wai as a young man back home in China. Once Saml started school, he soon changed his name to the more anglicised version of 'Sam', something he felt more comfortable with among his classmates. This emphasis on gaining a good education was later applied equally to the other children and, unlike circumstances back in China, the daughters, Doris and Gladys were also included, and they were encouraged to aspire for success and seize every educational opportunity that presented itself.

Meanwhile, with the passing of time, James Chue was beginning to feel that the workload and the daily responsibilities of his position as the Superintendent Missioner to the Chinese of Ballarat and regional Victoria were becoming too burdensome at his advanced age. In 1903 he notified the Presbyterian Church authorities that he wished to retire from his duties and return permanently to China, where he hoped to continue spreading the faith amongst his own countrymen and, true to the Chinese proverb, return to the soil of his native land as his final resting place. The White Australia Policy had been enacted in 1901 and many mature Chinese had then decided, like himself, that they preferred to return to the native villages of their ancestors to renew family connections. James was satisfied that he could confidently hand all the responsibilities of the mission to his friend and loyal assistant, John Tong Wai, who would faithfully continue his work into the future. Upon his departure, he was given a most appreciative farewell from his Chinese flock and the many members of the Ballarat East community he had served so faithfully since the opening of the Chinese Mission church so many years back. He was also acknowledged with a formal farewell ceremony by the Ballarat City Councillors.

LIFE AT
6 YOUNG STREET

After the fifteen years John had been working among the Little Bendigo Chinese, he and his family were now to be uprooted from their familiar surrounds with the prospect of a move to the Chinese Church and manse at number 6 Young Street, overlooking the site of the original Chinese village at Golden Point.

15. Church and Manse Young St

They faced the challenges of a new and larger community, with an established Chinese congregation formerly cared for over many years since 1883 by his predecessor Reverend James Chue (originally

Tang Chu), who was now turning 60 years of age and ready to vacate the position in favour of a younger man. Hence, John Tong Wai was duly appointed by the Presbyterian Church as the new Superintendent Missioner to Chinese in Ballarat and regional Victoria. He was to administer to the needs of his new Golden Point congregation, both spiritually and pastorally, but with responsibility beyond Ballarat to oversee the other five remaining centres, all of which had their own Chinese catechists with attendant duties to administer to the needs of surrounding Chinese populations concentrated in and around mining localities throughout country Victoria. At the time, these were at Warrnambool, Ararat, Beaufort, Beechworth and Geelong. This would mean he would be required to undertake regular trips further afield to maintain contact. John had arranged for the sale of his hut and land in Lofven Street, which was purchased by George Tew Wing, a local Chinese hawker, but the family was unable to move directly into the manse at 6 Young Street whilst James Chue still lived there awaiting his return trip home to China. To enable him to undertake the duties of his new position, John and the family were temporarily housed at the Joss property in Chinatown nearby at Golden Point. Every Sunday afternoon a strange but familiar sight to the local residents was the cavalcade of ageing Chinese men, mostly market gardeners, who shuffled along in single file with their hands customarily clasped behind their backs, making their way uphill from Barkly Street towards the Chinese Mission Church. Many of them were situated on the rich soil of the Yarrowee river flats beside the Sunnyside Woollen mill, living in crude, makeshift wooden huts, and reliant on selling their garden produce to the local community for their meagre living. Despite the fact that many of them attended the services of John Tong Wai, they had still not become converts to Christianity. Nevertheless, they continued to support him with their presence faithfully each week in appreciation for the many loyal deeds and pastoral care he carried out on their behalf as a fellow countryman.

At this stage, Saml was enrolled at the Golden Point State School where his younger siblings would also attend as they came of age. 'Sam', as he preferred to be called, was a bright student and keen to excel.

16. Golden Point State School

From the age of nine years he had piano lessons between 7.30 a.m. to 8.30 a.m. twice weekly, which enabled him to play the hymns in the Chinese church for the afternoon and evening services on Sundays. The day began with the 10.00 a.m., 11.00 a.m. and 2.00 p.m. services at St. John's Presbyterian Church in Peel Street, followed by 3.00 p.m in the Chinese Mission church at Young Street, then down to the Chinese Church in Main Road in the evening. Usually the attendances at this time were twenty to thirty, and these were mostly the elderly market gardeners. Sam remembered in later years that he felt somewhat apart from them as he could not converse with them because of language difficulties. He said he felt rather estranged and uncomfortable around them, and he considered that it had occurred because there was a status distinction between them, strengthened by his better education. He was an avid reader and borrowed from the St. John's Church library which he regarded as a treasure trove, and he also visited the Ballarat Public Library regularly. When, much later on, at thirteen years of age, he gained his merit certificate with good results, he was the only student from Golden Point to apply for a scholarship and he also enrolled at the School of Mines evening classes to study electricity and magnetism. Driven to excel, he attended these classes, sitting alongside Robert Menzies and subsequently, both students were successful in gaining scholarships. Sam was rewarded with a scholarship to continue his education at Ballarat High School, then known as Ballarat Agricultural College, whilst Robert Menzies was awarded a scholarship to attend Wesley College in Melbourne. Always highly motivated, Sam was quite proud of the fact that in 1909 he attended meetings for the Ironworker's Association. Although the youngest there, he wrote up the weekly talks for Monday's *Ballarat Courier* newspaper: this was because he claimed that he wished to broaden his education and widen his horizons among ordinary working chaps. He also undertook geological excursions on Saturday afternoons with an older friend, Professor Hart from the School of Mines. It was reported in the local *Courier* in 1914 that Sam had attended SMB, gaining a pass in the sign-writing exam, but for what purpose he never made completely clear.

It was strange how, at Golden Point and other local schools nearby where there was a significant number of 'half-caste' children enrolled, it was common practice that the family names of the Chinese inhabitants of Ballarat East were often changed and anglicised. This happened on the children's reports, in school rolls and in various everyday records from one year to the next. Eventually, the Tong Wai family also adopted the new spelling of Tong Way for common usage. Sam recalled that it first changed for him when he went on to Ballarat High School in 1908 and from that point in time the family had adopted it as well.

Ballarat Agricultural High School.

17. Ballarat Agricultural High School (old)

Life at number 6 Young Street was now extremely busy for Mary as well as her husband. She had a growing family to tend to, with the additional births of Alfred, Kenneth and Stephen in the following years to 1913. Discipline within the household was strict, but John Tong Way never hit his children. A stern, private word of admonishment was enough, supplied always by their mother. It was about this time that the decision was taken to transfer the younger children – Gordon, Alfred and Gladys – from Golden Point State school to Humffray Street and along with his siblings in 1913 young Kenneth also started in the infant grade.

The original Humffray St Primary School building, constructed in 1876.

18. Humffray St. School

The reason for this change was the fact that Humffray Street was still highly regarded as a scholarship school where they would have greater opportunities to complete their merit certificates and win scholarships to continue their education at a higher level. Due to the poor wage that John Tong Wai was paid by the Presbyterian Church as a Chinese minister, despite his ordination, the parents depended on their children being able to largely fund their own education. This focus on attaining scholarships was an important decision which bore fruit later on for Sam, Hedley, Doris, Kenneth and Gladys in particular as they all progressed to secondary education with excellent results. Proof of academic success was evidenced in 1913 when the results of the public service examinations were announced in the *Ballarat Star* newspaper, stating that Hedley Tong Way had qualified for a permanent clerical appointment. At this stage, Hedley was greatly pleased to be assured of secure, ongoing, respectable employment in a government position. For a full-blooded Chinese Australian particularly, this was the desired affirmation of acceptance and equality of opportunity they all sought.

Meanwhile, in the intervening years, tiny Mary Tong Wai had confronted her own challenges in a new, more densely-packed neighbourhood with houses directly next door, more people and much less privacy than she had experienced in Little Bendigo over the previous ten years. There was one positive consolation, which was the fact that she was now closer to her friend Jessie Jo Quong, who was living within walking distance further uphill from the manse at Mount Pleasant. They would be able to visit and see each other more often. Mary was still very housebound and rather reluctant to venture far from home, due to her inability to walk far, but Jessie often visited with her children, as evidenced in the photo of the manse, where Jessie is standing with her children in the foreground at the fence, with Mary just visible behind it in the background. Her English was still rather basic for conversation with Europeans who did not speak her own language, as she always conversed with her husband in Cantonese. She was a busy, devoted mother to her growing family with stepson Joseph, Sam, Hedley and Doris, plus young Gordon born in 1901 whilst still at Little Bendigo. It was not long after they settled at Young Street that she discovered she was with child again and happy to give birth to a second daughter they named Gladys, born on 29th June 1904. She was a bright and beautiful child, who displayed a sunny temperament and exceptional intelligence at an early age. She was fortunate to be enrolled at school in her early years at nearby Golden Point, and then, at grade three, to increase her opportunities she moved on to Humffray Street State School which still had a continuing reputation as a scholarship school for students with educational potential.

Clearly, John Tong Wai and his wife, Mary, were always very

keen to encourage their children to assimilate and do well with their education in order to succeed and gain acceptance in the predominantly WASP society of Ballarat. When they were young and living in the confines of the home, the children comprehended most of the spoken Chinese language between John and Mary, but they were strongly discouraged from speaking Chinese and did not acquire the spoken language themselves. As Sam would say many years later when he was quite elderly, 'We were not encouraged in the culture and so we grew away from the language. We considered ourselves as Australian, unlike our parents.' Without the language it is understandable why the subsequent Tong Way generations experienced disinterest in maintaining or celebrating any vestiges of a Chinese cultural identity. Mary understood intuitively that the children needed some freedom from the rigid expectations of her husband, the Reverend. In later years their grandson Stephen, who was Joseph's son, remembered how he longed to attend the local picture-show on a Saturday afternoon, despite the strong disapproval expressed by his grandfather. However, behind his back, Stephen's grandmother, Mary, took advantage of the times on a Saturday when John was away from home, by allowing her grandson to escape with a friend to see the show. Surreptitiously, he left home creeping via the side pathway so that he and his friend could not easily be observed in this act of disobedience, flaunting his grandfather's stated opinion about such frivolity. This act of complicity between grandmother and grandson was a significant step by Mary that demonstrated a considerable amount of courage and strength of character on her part, given the subsidiary role of complete obedience that was expected from a Chinese wife. Thankfully, Stephen was relieved that their secret was never discovered. Both he and his younger brother Michael always retained a special love for sweet Mary, their caring, understanding, little grandmother.

Over the intervening years all of the children had made their way successfully at school, also helping at home and attending a succession of prayer meetings and services in order to 'keep the Sabbath holy'. During their leisure hours at home, the boys sometimes mixed with non-Chinese or half-caste children in the immediate neighbourhood, but as Sam remarked during his later years, 'We mixed to some extent, but we had to remain a little aloof because of our father's position. We were the only Chinese family!'. He always regarded himself as different from the neighbourhood's 'half-caste' children in this respect. However, his brother Hedley had demonstrated considerable athletic ability and he was permitted to join the local amateur athletics club known as the Ballarat Harriers. It was conveniently located where the Llanberris Oval is today, just off Young Street and downhill from the manse. His sporting success at the long jump with a distance of 16 feet (4 metres) was reported in *The Australasian* in 1913 when he was seventeen, in addition to his other sprinting successes such as the Ballarat East Harriers Championships 100 reported in the *Ballarat Star* the same year. This enabled Hedley to participate locally with non-Chinese boys who shared a similar interest, and it therefore gave him a measure of freedom from the constant pressures at home. He also played the violin and on several occasions he and his sister Doris played a duo together in public performances, as reported in the *Ballarat Star* in 1908, and on another occasion they performed at the Daylesford Town Hall. However, it was far more restrictive for females. Compared with their brothers, Doris and her younger sister, Gladys, were not permitted anywhere near the same amount of freedom and spent most of their spare hours at home studying for school or helping their mother. Both Doris and young Gladys were extremely clever girls and due to the encouragement of both parents to aim for high academic standards, they succeeded in gaining the recognition of their teachers at an early age. Particularly high expectations were voiced on behalf of young Gladys as she was not only extremely clever, but much loved and admired by all who knew her; it was because of her sunny nature and considerate personality. She was a joy to her mother and a great help with many of the mundane chores about the house, avidly reading many books in her spare moments and sincerely embracing the simple teachings of her father's Christian faith.

19. Rare photo of Gladys (centre) surrounded by family

It was a sad fact that strangers, mostly children, but those who were not immediate neighbours in the Golden Point locality often threw small pebbles and laughed, calling hurtful verbal taunts at the Chinese market gardeners outside the mission church when they attended the services. The Tong Way family itself was now less exposed to this behaviour because of their higher status, better integration, and the measure of respect they had established in the local community. On any rare occasions of racism experienced, they had soon learnt to turn the other cheek. The proverb of 'sticks and stones will break my bones, but names will never hurt me' was a most relevant common mantra. However, in the village where the Chinese huts were located, vandalism was rife and there were many broken windows the Chinese could testify to as a result of the exploits of mischievous gangs of young boys. The Joss House in Main Road became a popular target for this form of entertainment. Despite her Asian appearance, Doris as the eldest girl in the family had learnt to cope by distancing herself and assuming an air of proud indifference which became her normal defence mechanism amongst her peers at school. She was academically bright and a high achiever by nature: it was this success that gave her visible proof and confidence in herself. To some fellow students like Jack Moy, a half-caste boy of Chinese descent from her neighbourhood who, like herself, had attained a good academic record at Golden Point State School and he also excelled as an athlete, she appeared very stand-offish and aloof. Both attended Ballarat High School and travelled along Sturt Street together by tram daily, but he recalled that they never really developed much friendly communication beyond a polite greeting. In Jack's opinion, he felt rather defensively that she saw herself as superior because she was not a half-caste, with both of her parents being pure Chinese and the father having an elevated position amongst them. Later on, Jack was to excel in athletics, and at the Bendigo Easter Fair in 1925 he became runner-up in the main event which was the Stawell Gift race, claiming he had been narrowly beaten 'by a hair's breadth'. But on another occasion, he proudly related how he won the Bendigo Gift at odds of 200:1 and with £201 as the first prize money! Jack always considered that he had been fortunate in gaining popularity and acceptance among his peers, mainly because of his sporting ability. As high achievers, both he and Doris were to become successful schoolteachers when they completed their education.

Jack Moy had a half caste mother, Maude Sang whose father was Lo Kwoi Sang and his father was a half-caste miner whose father was John Cullen Moy (Amoy). His Chinese grandfather, Cheng Moy, had once been a successful mine owner and formerly owned the hotel and half the town of Haddon (as related by Jack when he was interviewed by the author at 85 years of age).

After John's old friend and supervisor, James Chue, had taken his sad, final farewell of his many Ballarat friends, both Chinese and European, he was bound for the homeland after twenty-two faithful years of working in Victoria. The Tong Wai family were overjoyed to move into the more spacious rooms of the manse, and for John it was a pleasure to be situated right next door to his church and place of worship in the Golden Point neighbourhood, unlike at Little Bendigo. John had much earlier made the acquaintance of the Reverend Minister Inglis at the local St. John's Presbyterian Church in Peel Street where he attended for worship regularly with the family every Sunday; this in addition to the services he held at the mission church for his Chinese worshippers and supporters. Sundays were strictly devoted as a 'day of rest' by the entire family for the purpose of venerating the Lord. At home the strict family ritual began early in the morning with a good, cleansing wash, followed by morning prayers, then morning church service at St. John's Presbyterian Church situated a short downhill walk away in Peel Street. This was followed by a service for the Chinese market gardeners, herbalists and trades people at the Young Street Mission Church in the afternoon. Personal baths for the family were a luxury not allowed that day, and no public activity was permitted either. Sam remembered being firmly chastised by his father on one occasion when he was chopping some firewood to replenish the kitchen stove. During the weekdays there were prayers at night and grace was said by John Tong Wai at every meal, always spoken in Cantonese. Bible classes and English lessons for numbers of illiterate Chinese were conducted at the mission building in Main Road during weeknights, assisted by Mrs. Murray who was a dedicated supporter of the mission and its work for many years. As part of his current responsibilities, John was still frequently required to visit other Victorian mission stations at Brunswick, Beechworth, Warrnambool, Camperdown and Talbot to support the work of the catechists and conduct any baptisms, that reached a rather discouraging total of thirteen conversions over the twelve months to 1904, including Ballarat. In order to achieve this, he often walked long distances of up to fourteen miles to reach his destination, without adequate transport. This meant that his wife, Mary, and the children became used to his regular, long absences from home.

By now, John had acquired a great knowledge of growing herbs and vegetables, possibly from his early experience in the village of his birth or from the many Chinese market gardeners that had developed their own allotments at Little Bendigo as a source of alternative income from mining. Hence, at his new Golden Point address it was not long before John had found another useful outlet for his energies in the form of a much larger vegetable and herb garden. His rural farming origins came to the fore in a useful way because he terraced the vacant land beside the manse and planted many Chinese vegetables that they were able to use for the family meals; but more importantly, he planted additional herbs because, by now, John had developed an extensive knowledge about the healing properties of the traditional herbs used in Chinese medicines back home. He was able to treat simple ailments without resorting to the need for a doctor and it was not long before he was treating the poor, often overworked and undernourished Chinese labourers who had not succeeded on the earlier goldfields. They were the unfortunates who were unable to raise enough money to return to their families and home villages in China, and lived out their lonely, isolated existences without the prospect of return; they remained captives of their misfortune in an alien land. In Ballarat, some eked out an existence by growing vegetables and setting up their crude huts on the arable, rich alluvial soil of the river flats around the Yarrowee Creek and its many tributaries reaching out in different directions around the Ballarat district. Soon, it seemed that word had passed around that Reverend Tong Wai had successfully treated various ailments with his herbal potions, and he began to have queries from nearby residents of Golden Point who were non-Chinese. His patients were all unsolicited and came to him by word of mouth. There was often a knock at the door when John was away, and it was Mary who responded and was questioned about the possibility of an appointment to see if the reverend would be able to help cure some ailment or other. Now, Mary was very careful about how to handle this matter with delicacy and tact, especially when the request came from a female person. Privately, she would relay the information to him about the complaint and describe the symptoms in careful detail. If it was a female patient, he cautiously refused to make any physical examination with them as a matter of self-protection and principle. In his position, he was aware that, as a person of Chinese birth and Asian appearance, he could not be too careful, no matter how well respected he was in the local community.

He would gather a range of herbs from the garden – in some cases these would have been dried prior to their use and then he carefully weighed them on his extremely accurate, fine wooden gold-scales. He would ask Mary to add a quantity of water to the mixture and boil them up on the wood stove for the patient to take home with them and use as prescribed by him. For patients he met face to face, he would hold their wrist to feel their pulse, but did not touch their torso, asking many questions before making a diagnosis. For breast lumps, he would prepare a hot poultice and Mary would put the mixture on some lint and apply it to the woman's breast in private. For open wounds, he would gather cobwebs from the attic and apply them directly to the wound to stop the bleeding and assist healing. One regular Golden Point patient who recalled visiting him in her younger years was Mrs Ulrich who lived nearby and suffered regularly from severe migraine headaches. She had found no relief from the medicines prescribed by her own doctor, and, in desperation, she thought to act on information she had heard about the effective treatments John Tong Wai had used on one of her neighbours with amazing results. She explained her problem to Mary Tong Wai who told her to call in the following day after she had spoken with her husband that evening when he returned home. John recorded this observation about Mary in his diary: 'She is a true helpmate to me in every way'. Next day, Mrs Ulrich called and knocked at the front door of the manse to be invited inside, where Mary presented her with a long, thin bottle of pale yellowish fluid sealed with a small cork. It was peppermint oil. Mary told her that she must rub the oil on her temples to relieve the pain and increase the circulation whenever she had a migraine coming on. Mrs Ulrich claimed that this simple remedy gave her great relief over many years, and she always sang the praises of Reverend Tong Wai, along with the many other local residents who came to rely on his treatments. Many years later, my mother Nancy recalled how she was cured from suffering severe appendicitis attacks by being made to drink his special herbal treatments. He immediately collected some herbs from his garden, which her grandmother, Mary, boiled into a potion, then, despite her reluctance, he made her hold her nose to prevent her from vomiting it up and he made her drink every mouthful until it was gone. Miraculously, there were no further attacks of appendicitis again! More recently, with the eventual sale of the church land, the backyard was excavated where the mission church building existed before its removal and a new double storey house was built. A discovery was made of a discarded mineshaft that was filled with many discarded glass bottles that once held the peppermint oil and other remedies prescribed by John Tong Way during the years before 1949 when he retired.

The nearby home of the Stanhope family who lived at 31 Barkly Street (now 41 Barkly St.) backed directly onto the side of the Manse property.

20. 31 Barkly St. - Stanhope house

Both their yards adjoined a small back lane and the Tong Wais found them to be friendly neighbours, whose children sometimes met with their own children. Mr Stanhope kept pigeons and was always referred to by the Tong Wai children as 'the bird man'. The Stanhope's youngest child, Mabel, recalled the occasion at home when she walked into a glass door and cut her face rather badly with the shattered glass. It was Mary Tong Wai who attended her with the advice to keep spitting copious amounts of saliva onto her hands and applying as much saliva as she could on the wound. She also applied cobwebs to the child's face to hold the skin together and help it heal. Mabel, or 'Mabs' as she came to be known, claimed in later years that this treatment produced remarkable results with no scarring visible at all. Her mother, Mrs Stanhope, was a strong, well-built woman who often helped Mary cope with young Gordon when he took one of his epileptic fits. Because of his size, at these times he was very hard to control for such a small, diminutive person as Mary who was less than five feet tall. She insisted that Mary was to call on her at any time if she needed help handling him.

In the days when Mabs recalled knowing my mother, Nancy, the children from both families had some contact with each other, but especially with their rear neighbour, Miss Booth. She lived at the back via the side lane which ran past the mission church and manse and they often used to visit her through this back lane. Miss Booth was an elderly spinster lady with snowy white hair whom they regarded as very religious and also extremely kind. The children loved to visit her, especially when she would make up some scone dough into 'mice' for them. In front of her house there was a large mulberry tree they loved to climb, especially when the berries were in season, returning home with stained hands and often the stains were all over their clothing as well. It was rumoured that Miss Booth was tragically 'spinstered' by the war when her sweetheart was killed in action. Almost reminiscent of a Dickensian tale, one day she showed Mabs the contents of her chest of drawers in the bedroom, containing her wedding dress and veil, wedding invitations and piles of his letters that she had kept. She confided that her sweetheart died from a sniper's bullet on the last day of the Boer War; tragically, they were soon to have wed. She mourned him all her life and never contemplated marrying anyone else. In later years as adults, the children from both families recalled her in their memories with great fondness and they spoke of the sympathy they had felt for her personal tragedy. On many occasions she was known to have fostered other young children temporarily; those who had lost their parents through tragic circumstances and were reduced to poverty or neglect.

21. Photo Miss Booth & Mrs Stanhope

In effect, John Tong Wai felt a strong obligation to heal his congregation and other members of his community spiritually, but also to heal their ailments and minister to their pastoral needs of everyday life when it was required of him. He regularly received the letters and written material on behalf of his fellow Chinese who were predominantly illiterate, uneducated peasants, mainly from the Sze Yap district in Kwangtung province. He wrote their letters and read their correspondence to them, also attending to their banking and other matters such as paying their fines or representing them in court whenever necessary. After the Sunday service in the mission church, he would gather with some of them in the front room of the manse over a cup of tea that Mary had prepared in the kitchen, and he would attend to their problems. In this regard, he acted as a buffer for the less fortunate members of his pastoral community and, as a consequence, he continued to be highly regarded by them. Attendances at the Chinese Mission Church in Little Bendigo and also at Golden Point had been consistently high prior to 1901 before the White Australia Policy was enacted. From this period on, they considered that their future potential in the country was now more limited and less secure. The opportunity to become normal, naturalised citizens was now impossible and they could no longer anticipate bringing their Chinese wives out to join them. Consequently, some of the more successful men who could afford the fare back home decided to return. Many of these were the herbalists who practiced in Peel Street, Main Road and other central locations near the Chinese community of Ballarat East along with other mining townships throughout Victoria where all returned to their homeland. They were thereby depleting the numbers of John's congregation and that of the catechists in areas under his charge quite significantly and almost overnight. From that point in time, the doors of Australia were closed to all Chinese wishing to enter the country and the prospect of naturalisation and citizenship was permanently denied those who remained.

Despite the fact that each year very few of the Ballarat Chinese had converted to Christianity, the remaining group of mostly aged market gardeners continued to struggle uphill to regularly attend services at the mission church: it was a symbol of their continued loyalty, respect and support for the work of John Tong Wai. Even in their old age, they did not fully relinquish their cultural ties but continued to worship in their traditional manner at the Chinese Joss as well.

22. Photo of Ballarat Joss house 1955

They contributed financially to John's work and often supported many charitable causes in the Ballarat community that he brought to their attention, such as the work of the Benevolent Asylum and raising money for the Ballarat hospital. In earlier years, there were some unfortunate Chinese men who had contracted leprosy and they were greatly feared and shunned by all others. Due to superstitious accusations by many Europeans in the community, they were often seen as a source of contamination and blamed for any outbreaks of disease. Consequently, the poor leper victims had been ostracised by the community to live on the outskirts of Ballarat East in Clayton Street, where they were forced to rely on the scraps of food and handouts that were donated and delivered to them by the Benevolent Society. As time went by, their numbers dwindled due to old age and lack of medical care, plus the effects of the disease and their poor living conditions.

The Tragedy of Loss

In the daily lives of Reverend Tong Way and his wife, Mary, whilst administering to the cares and concerns of others they regarded as less fortunate, they were to encounter much sorrow, personal care and loss of their own. Death soon became a shadowy presence which lurked within the manse household, taking its toll all too often in the years which preceded and heralded the aftermath of the First World War. Tragedy first struck on 2nd October 1917 with the death of their youngest child, Stephen, from tubercular meningitis at only four years of age. The small coffin was lovingly prepared and his small body, wearing his Sunday best outfit, was laid out in the front room amidst the many tears and final prayers of farewell by the family, then later lovingly carried from the family residence for the final journey. Its heavy-hearted coffin bearers were the older brothers Sam and Hedley. A sad procession, with the twelve pall bearers, ten of whom were Chinese, proceeding into the Ebenezer Church where Reverend D. W. Smith conducted the service, largely attended by many mourners. But in these times, young deaths were not a rare occurrence and life must go on, despite the aching hearts and the grief. Mary did not attend, but she grieved in private and visited the grave at the Ballarat New Cemetery separately with her daughter the following day. This public absence of the mother was accepted as being quite a customary cultural practice among the Chinese congregation in Ballarat.

It was in 1920 that the Tong Way household was stricken with tragedy once again, when young Alfred came down with consumption at only thirteen years of age. Despite the desperate attempts of Mary to nurse her child and treat him with every herbal medicine that John could devise, it was to no avail. Sadly, he succumbed to this disease and weakened before his mother's anxious, heartbroken gaze until his eyes closed for the last time. On the large dining table in the front room, dressed in his best Sunday outfit, he lay in his small coffin within the manse in readiness for his final journey; to be carried aloft with heavy hearts once again by his two eldest brothers, Sam and Hedley. Grief stricken and inconsolable, Mary stayed at home as before; she would once again visit the grave with her daughters to mourn in privacy later on.

In a cruel stroke of fate, the agony of loss was to be compounded for the Tong Way family only one year later on, as their treasured, beautiful daughter, Gladys, came down suddenly on a Saturday morning in June 1921 with a severe chill and a fever: a condition that rapidly worsened before the helpless ministrations of Mary and the doctor who attended her over that weekend. Despite all frantic efforts, tragically and so suddenly, she died early in the morning the following day. John Tong Way found himself helpless, as on this occasion he had no herbal remedies which could offer a solution: the death certificate listed the diagnosis as incurable meningitis. Poor Mary suffered an agony of grief at losing her loving daughter and special soul mate at such a young age; and one who had promised so much for the future. It was enough to break the spirit of any mother who had lost so many at such an early stage of life.

In the *Ballarat Star* newspaper there appeared a lengthy and moving personal obituary, which described Gladys as 'an accomplished and clever young lady of seventeen years' with the added mention that she 'was a student of the Technical school and had obtained a scholarship and was giving promise of great achievement and was a favourite with all who knew her, because of her bright and cheerful temperament'. This article gave testament to the shock and sense of bereavement felt by a large part of the local Golden Point community who had come in contact with her over her short lifetime. It was a huge funeral held at the Chinese Presbyterian Mission Church, with tearful representatives from her school, both students and teachers, plus scholars from the Chinese Mission, St John's Peel Street Presbyterian Church, St. Andrew's Kirk, and numerous others. It was described as 'impressive' and a 'touching testimony of the sympathy of the people with the bereaved in the loss of one so much beloved and respected.' Once again, the two elder brothers, Sam and Hedley, were coffin-bearers with the heartrending task of carrying their beloved younger sister to her final resting place. They were aided by two Chinese scholars from the mission school, Ah Cet and George Grey, who were family friends and had known her well. All of the lady teachers, classmates and scholars of the mission walked in a long procession at the cemetery from the entrance to the graveside where Reverend Cloyd officiated. A long and detailed list of local dignitaries who attended was included in the obituary on the following Thursday 30th June following the funeral. Stricken with her grief, Mary once again remained at the manse in Young Street and attended the graveside to mourn privately in company with her elder daughter, Doris, the following day.

Some members of the family consider that she never fully recovered from the pain of this particularly bitter loss.

On the twenty-second of February 1934, exactly 33 years to the date of his birth, their son Gordon became desperately ill with an acute gastric attack that he did not survive. Because he was a chronic epileptic and took regular fits, his constant need for special care had taken a serious toll on his mother's health, so that she had developed a weak heart. Although the death certificate had verified his death from an acute gastric attack, there was an element of doubt rumoured among family members. Some considered that he had been permitted to pass away due to the continual strain placed on his mother's health due to his severe epilepsy over the past thirty-three years. It was considered that in some respects it was a blessing, because his condition would worsen as he advanced in years and the demands on his mother would have been extreme. Always a likeable personality and cheerful by nature, he had not completed his education beyond grade six. Although enrolled at Humffray Street school, he did not continue with a secondary education as his older brothers had done. He lived permanently at home with his parents for his entire life, largely dependent on Mary's constant care and surveillance. Physically, he was always extremely strong, large and hard to handle during one of his frightening turns. Many of the neighbours, including Mrs Stanhope next-door, remarked at the amazing resilience of his mother in coping for so long. Hence the funeral of Gordon Tong Way, the second youngest surviving son, well known and regarded sympathetically in the local community, took place on a Thursday, with a large attendance of friends and sympathisers and ladies interested in the mission. A great collection of beautiful wreaths and floral tributes had been placed on the coffin and an impressive service was held in the Mission Church at Young Street, conducted by Reverend J. A. Moscript of the St John's Presbyterian Church in Peel Street. Some of Gordon's favourite hymns, 'What a Friend We Have in Jesus' and 'Jesu Lover of My Soul', were sung with raised voices by all. Once again, the six coffin bearers included his older brothers, Sam and Hedley Tong Way, plus a Mr Robertson and three Chinese friends of the family Ah Din, Yet Way and a Mr Ping. Amongst the pallbearers there were an additional ten Chinese names listed in the newspaper.

Now, young Kenneth, as the baby of the family, was considered to have had good fortune smile upon him, because he was not only good looking, but with a sensitive, gentle and warm personality.

23. Photo of Kenneth Tong Wai

It meant that he was a favourite with all family members and all those who came in contact with him as he grew into manhood. Everyone loved this young, sweet natured man called Kenneth, including my mother, Nancy! He was scholarly, like his older brothers, and at twenty-four years of age he was expected to make his mark at whatever became his chosen profession. Like his brother Sam and sister Doris, he decided to make teaching his choice and his future seemed secure. In 1934 he began his teaching career, but unforeseen events intervened. It came as a huge blow when Kenneth was seriously weakened by what was thought to be a leaking valve of the heart. He had only been teaching for a short couple of years, when suddenly he became ill. Despite her loving care, to his mother's despair, his condition worsened dramatically until he was so weak that he was bedridden for several weeks before sadly, in March 1936, aged only 25 years old, he died as his entire family stood heartbroken and helplessly by. One can imagine the intense grief for Mary the mother, having to witness the loss of yet another cherished child of her womb dying so inexplicably at such a young age. Death seemed to be ever present in the fortunes of this God loving family! Once again, another funeral for Reverend Tong Way's family took place at the Chinese Presbyterian Mission Church in Young Street on Tuesday 24th March 1936 at the conclusion of a brief service for this dearly loved youngest son. It was followed by the solemn journey to the place of internment at the Ballarat New Cemetery. This recent tragic loss, compounded by the preceding deaths, took its toll on the family, particularly on Mary, whose health was rapidly failing under the stress created by all the terrible grief and anxiety she had experienced over past years. Apart from the eldest three surviving children born at Little Bendigo, the following six children had all died during the years spent living at the manse in Young Street. Mary was never prone to making any complaints or raising attention to the state of her ailments, so her long-suffering tendencies meant that her daily duties as a wife and mother were largely overlooked and taken for granted by the family. She became even more housebound as her strength was severely tested in subsequent years following this latest death.

THE WAR YEARS INTERVENED

As the eldest child of John and Mary, Sam was perhaps the most driven to prove himself as a worthy citizen of Australia by excelling in his chosen profession of teaching. Early on he had rejected his father's encouragement to follow in his footsteps and become a minister of the church. He had also rejected his second suggestion of joining a bank. His sights were set on a teaching career which offered him in his eyes a guaranteed position of respectability. After Sam had completed his two years at Ballarat Agricultural High School in 1912, he became a student teacher, firstly at Dean Higher Elementary School, approximately ten miles from Ballarat, then in the same year he transferred to his old school, Humffray Street, closer to home. He then sat the state-wide exams for the first secondary teacher studentships to be awarded and in 1914 he was one of the first teachers to complete a two-year diploma course and graduate for secondary teaching from Teachers' College at Melbourne University. Of the twelve students; seven girls and five boys, Sam was the only person of Chinese-Australian-born descent. During this time, he thoroughly enjoyed the freedom of his life, away from the constraints and expectations of, particularly, his father in Ballarat. With his distinctive Asian features and short stature, he was fortunate in being good looking and clever. He consciously strived to become assimilated and accepted by dint of his academic achievements and his eagerness to socialise and mingle with like-minded, upwardly mobile 'white' achievers whom he identified with. He claimed that he had 'broadened out' so that whilst in Melbourne he had nothing to do with fellow Chinese and he did not attend church services where he would be in contact with any. As a boy one remembers that he claimed he had always felt 'somewhat apart' from his fellow Chinese and he found communication with them difficult, as he considered that he had 'developed away from them'. As time went on, he became more distanced from his ethnic origins in his bid for success and self-identification. It was Hedley who became the first to gain permanent employment, when he sat the public service entry exam. He had a mathematical flair for figures and, unlike Sam, he was happy to have a lower profile in a secure, reasonably well-paid government position – an occupation that left him free to pursue his other recreational interests, such as playing the violin, the sport of hunting, and having a bit of a fling at the races. The two brothers were nothing alike in personality and those who knew them at this time described them so differently. Sam was considered the better looking, but Hedley was more easy-going or self-effacing and took himself less seriously.

It was whilst Sam was in a student teaching position at the Higher Elementary School in Clunes township near Ballarat later on that the outbreak of war was declared. Despite the interruption to his teaching career, Sam was eager to enlist as he considered it his duty as an Australian born citizen to help defend the country. In 1915 a friend from Ballarat had already joined up and others followed. At the time Sam enlisted to join the armed services in 1916, he remembered going to the training camp, but to his surprise several weeks later, he claimed that without explanation he was apprehended and marched to the St Kilda barracks for questioning. To his extreme disappointment and embarrassment, he was subsequently informed that he was rejected on the basis that he 'didn't have enough European blood' and because, at that stage, China had not entered the war. He received a formal letter of explanation which thanked him, but he was extremely upset about it. Similarly, his brother Hedley was also rejected when he applied. Once more, still undaunted, both brothers re-enlisted in 1916 for a second try when conscription came up, but they were again unsuccessful. Sam was told this time that he had hammer toes, but Hedley was also rejected because of his obvious 'Chinese blood'. Being extremely upset and embarrassed at his rejection, Sam felt that he could not face his return to the school at Clunes, as he had previously been given such a rousing send-off by the school staff and local community. He successfully applied for a transfer and took up another teaching position at Daylesford Higher Elementary School. It was whilst teaching there that, early in 1917, he enlisted once more and was finally accepted into the Australian Medical Corps. Only nine days before him, Hedley had also enlisted and this time he had been accepted into the 3rd Divisional Signal Company as a sapper with the rank of private.

24. Hedley and Sam in uniform

In terms of Hedley and Sam's earlier rejections and the success of their third attempt at enlistment, the situation had altered over the length of the war with public awareness of the shocking casualty lists which had tarnished the glorious notion of 'Duce et Decorum Este': the numbers of new recruits were fast diminishing as time went on. Also by now, China had entered the war, so in their case a special exemption was granted despite their Chinese blood. For the parents, John and Mary, the situation was different: they were pacifists and became unhappy at their sons' enthusiasm to enlist. Thus, before Sam and Hedley were rejected the first time, John Tong Way had tried unsuccessfully to intervene and dissuade them against joining the armed forces on the basis of his religious, pacifist beliefs. Sam had made his feelings very clear to his father before his second attempt to join up and his parents finally accepted that their children felt a different identification towards Australia as their homeland and did not share the divided loyalties of their parents. As Sam later explained about his parents, in his opinion, 'they didn't have my feelings for Australia'. However, as native-born Chinese who were only partially accepted, it is understandable that they did not fully identify themselves as true citizens of Australia.

A diary titled *The Story of My Life* recently came to my attention when I was contacted by Jordan Gregory, the great grandson of a soldier who served in WW1 with my own grandfather Hedley. The soldier's name was William Alan Watkins who was also in the same army training camp at Seymour with Hedley. In the diary account, William related his surprise when Hedley first began his active service in the training camp, and he explains how Hedley encountered this element of racism directed toward his Chinese appearance. It is evident in the personal reaction of William himself as a fellow soldier when he made the following remark: 'Good Heavens, a bloomin Chow in the Batt'. It was a sharp indication of the prejudice Hedley would regularly encounter and would need to overcome. However, William's diary recorded the fact that he soon changed his mind completely when they were both thrown together to undertake a task at the railway station and found it necessary to communicate with each other. William mentioned his complete surprise at how unexpectedly well-spoken Hedley seemed, thus indicating that he was very well educated and civilised. Ironically, following this encounter, they formed a strong bond of friendship throughout their training, and it continued for many years after their war experience ended. Over their training period they spent much time together socially, and Hedley spent weekends staying at William's family home, because travel to his Ballarat home was time consuming and so far distant. As his grandchild, the recent knowledge I acquired from reading the diary about this friendship led to a subsequent revelation: a photograph that was in my possession, of Hedley seated alongside an unknown 'white' soldier had always been in the collection of the Tong Way family since the war ended. Now, happily, the mystery has been finally solved, because I sent William's great grandson a copy and he was able to identify Hedley's companion as his own great grandfather, William Alan Watkins.

25. Photo of Hedley and William Watkins

Later, whilst in France and serving in action, Hedley was promoted to the rank of Extra Regimental 2nd. Corporal with the 5th Australian Divisional Signal Company. Both of the Tong Way brothers had ended up in the same 5th division when Sam transferred from the Medical Corps: this was due to the physical rigors of stretcher bearing being unsuited to his small physical stature, as he was only five foot three inches tall. Unlike Hedley, who had already seen action in France, Sam remained at the rank of private and saw no action for the remainder of the war, as he was posted much later to France, arriving just after the Armistice was signed. However, ambitious and always alert for every opportunity, he then obtained a scholarship for a year's extended leave from the AIF to attend the Imperial College of Science in London, studying physics and chemistry. The following year, in 1920, he returned to Australia to complete a final subject in political economy at Melbourne University before once more embarking on his teaching career at Williamstown High School. He was working part-time whilst completing a Bachelor of Arts degree and graduated in 1921.

26. Photo of Sam Tongway's graduation

When Ballarat's Arch of Victory was created as a memorial to the soldiers of the First World War, the female workers from the Ballarat Lucas Factory planted an extensive line of trees to create the Avenue of Honour on the western side of Ballarat. It included two young trees with a name-plaque for both brothers Sam and Hedley, each planted and erected on the same day, 9th June 1919, and beside which they later proudly posed for a photograph.

27. Photo of Sam's avenue tree and plaque

In the aftermath of WW1, Hedley once again sat the exam successfully to enter the employment of the public service as a clerk, but when he heard that he may be able to apply for a soldier settlement block, he went ahead and registered an application. He had the romantic notion that he would enjoy being on some land of his own, but in truth, it was a rather unrealistic fantasy, as he was small in stature, lightly built and his lungs had been affected by the poisonous gas from being in the trenches during the war; he suffered frequently from emphysema. However, he was delighted to hear that he had been successful in gaining an allotment of land in the Trawalla Estate Soldier Settlement at Lake Goldsmith in the county of Ripon, four miles from Beaufort and twenty-four miles from the Ballarat Railway station. It was regarded as land suitable for grazing and mixed farming. The conditions determined payment in six-monthly instalments over a term of thirty-six and a half years, with the lessee required to reside on his allotment until the land became freehold. The only way these conditions could be waived was in the case of sickness or adverse circumstances, whereby a transfer could be made with the consent of the board. Hedley had no prior experience or knowledge about farming, so he was ill equipped for the life of a farmer, particularly because he was a bachelor and had no family close by. The land he was allocated included an area of 340 acres in the Parish of Yangerahwi. Nevertheless, although Hedley lacked farming experience, he quickly made contact with other property owners in the district and joined in many of the local community groups. He was easy going by nature and had a great interest in horse racing, being a bit of a gambler according to his brother Sam who frequently expressed his disapproval. Also, he became a member of the Masonic Lodge, which enabled him to make friendships and helpful contacts that he could use to his benefit when necessary to ask for advice and help. The people of Goldsmith had welcomed him into their community, and he experienced no prejudice against his Chinese appearance at all. He became a popular personality in the closely-knit township and many men came to his aid with their farming advice and assistance, because he was 'having a go'. Also, his war experience and the fact that he had voluntarily enlisted and fought for his country of birth, irrespective of his Chinese parentage, was an added factor in becoming liked, respected and accepted in the district.

He worked hard over the next couple of years to establish himself as a farmer, but eventually he was forced to face the fact that he was fighting a losing battle on the land. He was not built for the daily physical demands of the life required of a farmer and his acreage was not large enough for him to make a comfortable living. He knew his lungs were not improving and the emphysema was getting worse, so reluctantly, he made the decision to apply for a transfer on health grounds. When he informed his friends, they were all genuinely regretful that he must go as he had won their friendship. However, they were not prepared to see him go without a rousing farewell celebration from the community, which was subsequently written up in the local paper. He humbly refused the offer of a formal civic farewell, but gladly attended a warm, more personal farewell held in a private home amongst friends. Fond speeches were made to express genuine regret at his leaving the community and he was presented with a generous gift to remember them by. Ironically, it seems he was a 'glutton for punishment', because soon afterwards, with financial help from his brother Sam, they invested their war savings and he took up what seemed more fertile land at Dean, much closer to Ballarat. At this time, it needed a lot of clearing as it was overgrown with blackberries and required a huge amount of manual labour, according to Sam. Sadly and perhaps predictably, it was another project doomed to financial failure and the aspirations of a farming life were permanently abandoned, despite the rich volcanic soil. Ironically, today it is occupied by wealthy farming families that have lived and prospered on this land for many generations and where farming continues.

Hedley loved to follow the horses and he also loved to go hunting when the opportunity arose. Among family photographs, he once showed a black and white photo of himself with gun in hand at a time when he went wild pig hunting up north. When holidaying with my grandparents at Torquay one year, I remember my grandmother Evelyn being upset with him for trapping rabbits, stating how cruel it was to bring them back wounded and still alive. Conversely, he had a much gentler side as he loved music and, to my child's ears, he played the violin rather well. In their double story home in Barkers Road he often disappeared upstairs, practicing by himself in isolation from the rest of the household; I used to creep up to sit on the stairs and I loved to listen to him playing during my time living with them from the age of three. Throughout his life, he loved to attend musical performances at every opportunity. Unfortunately, my grandmother failed to appreciate and share this musical interest with him, although she did like to follow the horse racing and demonstrated a canny knack for picking the winners. She always liked to see if she had chosen the winning horse; something she did many a time, but strangely, without ever placing a bet. Years later, when Hedley met up with his future second wife, Gladys, whilst living in Adelaide, their acquaintanceship began with a shared music interest: this occurred when they were regularly seated next to each other because of the season tickets they had purchased for an orchestral concert series.

On a very determined note, Sam often said that his main aim in life was to integrate fully into the community where he lived. 'I took as my stand that I was a citizen of the country. I had fought for the country and therefore I should work for the country as well.' He claimed that he had enlisted to show his gratitude. He was 'concerned for the moral uplift' of the country. He reiterated that he had not taken up any aspect of his parent's culture because he was 'educated away from it.' He proudly stated that he was 'never in touch with culture from China' but he had made himself an educated citizen of Australia without the knowledge of other countries. At the time, he appeared extremely proud of the fact that he had proved himself by totally rejecting his ethnic origins with the exclusion of all else as a measure of his 'Australianness'. To all appearances, Sam was indeed a good, upstanding, and professionally successful member of the communities in which he lived and worked, but it seemed that it was at the cost of being unable to acknowledge or celebrate with pride the rich heritage of his Chinese parents and their ancient culture. It appeared that this was the price they paid for their assimilation and acceptance, because Hedley also displayed little interest in learning or celebrating any aspect of his Asian heritage. Although he was successful in his chosen career of clerical work for the postal service, unlike Sam, he seemed to be less concerned about his public image and not so eager to maintain the trappings of social recognition; he was simply prepared to live life with all its foibles as it came to him. It is interesting to note that much later, during the early stages of the 1939-45 war, both Sam and Hedley, driven by a sense of obligation and loyalty, became involved in serving their country once again. Sam gained the honorary rank of Flying Officer, teaching mathematics and science to young men in the Air Training Corps. Hedley also re-enlisted for behind-the-scenes military service, where he was based in Westgarth, Victoria throughout the war until 1945. Sam later joined the RSL wherever he was teaching, and proudly marched every Anzac Day without fail, until a year before his last birthday at 93 years, when he was too ill and became a seated observer. He considered one of his greatest achievements was to be awarded a life membership of the Australian Natives Association.

AUSTRALIAN NATIVES' ASSOCIATION
Merbein Branch No. 272

NATIONAL BENEFIT
EDUCATIONAL
LITERARY
AUSTRALIAN IDEALS
PATRIOTISM

ESTABLISHED
MAY 30TH 1921
POST OFFICE BOX 12
PHONE MERBEIN

JNO. W. MARROWS, Secretary

Merbein.
July 7th, 1949.

S. J. Tongway, Esq.,
Head Master, S. S.
Violet Street,
Bendigo.

Dear Mr. Tongway,-

At a recent meeting of the Merbein Branch of the A. N. A., during a discussion on the progress of the Merbein District Children's Library (in which the members of the Branch continue to be interested) mention was made of the fact that the initial steps which led to the eventual formation of the Library were taken by the A. N. A., at the instigation of your good self.

As as result of the discussion, members expressed their desire to, in some small way, pay tribute to the work you had acomplished during your stay in Merbein.

I was instructed, therefore, to ask if you would accept from the members of the Branch, a Life Honorary Membership in the Association and Branch. Such a Life Honorary Membership carries with it membership in the Association and Branch for the lifetime of the member, without the payment of any dues or contributions of any kind.

The members of the Merbein A. N. A. recognise that such a membership can be of little or no intrinsic value to your good self, but they instruct me to say that they would feel honored if you would acceed to their request, thus enabling them to feel that you were still an honored member of the Merbein Branch.

I am forwarding a declaration which, should you be disposed to agree to our request, I shall be glad if you will sign and return to me at your convenience.

Kind regards to Mrs. Tongway and all best wishes to your good self.

Yours Fraternally,-

Jno. W. Marrows, Secretary, Merbein Branch A. N. A.

SUPPORT YOUR COUNTRY, AND IT WILL SUPPORT YOU

28. ANA membership certificate photo

He would proudly display the certificate and on one of my visits he brought it out to show me and allowed me to make a copy of it. I was struck by a certain irony in the situation, given that it was an organization that celebrated being of European descent, but I understood how important this acknowledgement had been to him as an Asian Australian.

New Challenges for the Family

I n January 1921, John Tong Way belatedly came to an important
decision and made the necessary application to become a naturalised
citizen of his adopted country, Australia.

29. John and Mary photos (headshots)

He was supported by a letter from John Walker, the minister of St.
Andrew's Kirk in Ballarat, commending him for his character and
long-standing service to the church. However, despite acknowledging
his worthiness, the response from the Commonwealth Government
to additional representations from Senators W. K. Bolton and T.
J. E. Bakhap on his behalf were firmly in the negative, due to the

White Australia Policy. The reason being given that 'Ever since the Commonwealth took control of the business of naturalisation in1904 it has been the policy not to naturalise Chinese, and although the form of the law has been recently changed and the policy has undergone some modifications, no change has yet been made in regard to dealing with applications by Chinese.' The letter was dated 26th April 1921 from the Commonwealth of Australia, the Senate. Surprisingly, Thomas Bakhap had succeeded to become a Senator in what was a most unusual occupation given his background, because he was the first person with Chinese links to be elected to an Australian parliament. His adoptive father was Chinese, his mother European, and he served in the Tasmanian Upper house from 1913 to 1927. Despite his continued representation on John Tong Way's behalf dated 7th October 1922, the correspondence continued in the negative on 10th October 1922'. It appears that despite his undoubted sympathy with John Tong Way's situation, even Senator Bakhap could not influence any change in the decision to reject his application. Mary Tong Way was less certain about making an application, but she also applied with encouragement from her husband, and she was met with the same resistance. John Tong Way persevered doggedly, with successive letters and endorsements from his referees between 1921 and 1922 but to no avail. Despite his impeccable reputation and his many years of selfless work in the Ballarat community, he was unsuccessful. He and his wife Mary would continue to have the uncertain status of aliens for the remainder of their lives in Australia, which was a bitter blow considering the sacrifices they had made by choosing to remain and raise their children to be Australians.

Surprisingly, many records falsely assume that he was naturalised and even his adult children believed that he had become naturalised. It was possibly an embarrassment and something that was never revealed or discussed by the parents. As late as the year before her death, Mary was still compelled to make an application for renewal of her Aliens certificate.

Decemb 16/9/41

COMMONWEALTH OF AUSTRALIA.

National Security (Aliens Control) Regulation

Form of Application for Registrati

(For Alien Resident in Australia)

This form is to be filled up (except as to signature and fi
triplicate, and the Alien is to attend in person, with the triplica
the member of the Police Force in charge of the Police Station nearest to his
usual place of abode, and, in his presence, sign the application and allow an
impression of his finger prints to be taken if required.

Name (in full) __WAY Mary Tong__ *(Surname to be underlined.)*

Nationality   Chinese   Sex   Female

Birthplace   Hong Kong   Date of Birth   3/3/1873

Place of abode   6 Young Street Ballarat East

Place of business (if any)   Nil

Occupation   Domestic duties   Married *(Strike out the term that does not apply.)*
                                  XXXXX
Date of entry into Australia   1893

Name of Ship   Unknown

Port of Debarkation   Melbourne

PERSONAL DESCRIPTION.

Height 5 ft.   in.   Colour of eyes Brown

Colour of Hair   Grey   Build   Medium

Notable marks

REMARKS

Finger prints—   Date of Application   23/9/39
(Impression to be made, if required, in presence of Aliens Registration Officer.)
Left hand   Right hand sual signature of alien *M. T. Toy*
                               (To be signed in presence of Registration Officer.)

(This space for office use only.)

Certificate issued—No. 7

Date   23/9/39

Remarks

                              Sergt 5344
Signature of Aliens Registration Officer.

                              Poli Ballarat East

30. Alien application form for Mary

Ironically, the granddaughter of the Quong family recently related how her grandfather Peter Quong managed to circumvent this situation of denial by illegally purchasing a naturalisation certificate from a former immigrant Chinese returnee to China. Peter changed his family name accordingly in order to purchase land and thus become the recipient of extra citizenship benefits and freedoms denied to John and Mary Tong Way as unnaturalised residents. This gives a possible explanation as to why the close friendship shared between the two families did not continue in later years. John Tong Way would have strongly disapproved of Peter Quong's actions and may have pressured Mary to discontinue the close friendship they had shared. Prior to the restrictions that arose from the White Australia Policy in 1901, it had been possible earlier for some resident Chinese to become naturalised, but the door was now permanently closed to all, no matter how long they had resided in the country.

Not only had John and Mary Tong Way raised a large family and tended to the cares and needs of the Chinese community in a spirit of Christian charity, but in 1928 they had undertaken a further burden of responsibility. Their son Hedley had married my grandmother, a white woman of Irish descent named Evelyn Maria Scanlon, born on a struggling potato farm in the swampy ground of Koo-wee-rup. They had met on an arranged outing as a matter of mutual convenience. Evelyn was working as a housemaid in a poorly paid position; she found it difficult to meet eligible young men, mainly because she was regarded as a 'fallen woman' due to having given birth to my mother, an illegitimate child born out of wedlock. Hedley also experienced rejection. He found his Chinese appearance was a great handicap when meeting young, eligible women socially; therefore, he was eager to continue courting young Evelyn, despite her hesitation. When on her day off she plucked up her courage and invited him to accompany her on a visit to see her six-year-old daughter at the orphanage, he agreed willingly. Upon their arrival, he was immediately horrified at the feverish and wasted condition the child was in and later that day he arranged for a doctor to attend her at the orphanage. Possibly influenced by his Christian upbringing and the companionship they had formed, he decided to propose marriage to Evelyn on the understanding that he was prepared to adopt her illegitimate daughter Nancy. When Evelyn accepted his proposal, Nancy was immediately removed from the orphanage. She was a sickly child, due to the appalling conditions of the home she had been raised in from the age of four years, and the situation had arisen because, with a fatherless child, Evelyn was constantly refused paid work, and without the means to survive, she could not afford to keep her child with her any longer.

31. Photo of young Nancy and mother Evelyn

Evelyn and Hedley decided that, due to the state of Nancy's health and because she was resentful and did not respond well to her natural mother, it was best to place her in the care of her adoptive grandparents, John and Mary Tong Way in Ballarat. It was on the understanding that it would be better for her to stay with them until she had fully recuperated, and it would allow time for Hedley and

Evelyn to settle into their newly married life when they would feel better able to take care of her. Hedley was now employed in a secure position by the Postal Department and was able to support the child financially, so this was not the problem. Whilst living in Ballarat, young Nancy's health improved and she settled in well. For the first time she was in a normal family situation and included in all domestic and religious activities as a member of the large Tong Way family. She responded to the love and care of her adoptive grandmother Mary in particular, for whom she developed a strong affection. It was at this time that her rebellious behaviour greatly improved. As a visibly 'white child' she found that no distinctions were made and she took part in all services held each Sunday at the Chinese Mission Church and eventually learnt to play the organ to accompany the regular hymns which this strange, elderly Chinese congregation sang in their rather querulous, sing song tones. At the time, she was blissfully unaware of the extremely unique situation she was in; a white child living in a Chinese household and being exposed daily to the comings and goings of the Chinese community. As a child she found that Grandfather Tong Way was kind, but strict and far more aloof in his role as the family disciplinarian and provider than her tiny, caring grandmother. However, she often claimed in later years that she remembered it was Grandfather Tong Way who came to the rescue with his miraculous herbal cure when she was suffering the acute pains of appendicitis and for this, she remained forever grateful.

In 1930 a daughter was born to Hedley and Evelyn: a stepsister for Nancy. She was christened Doris Winifred after Hedley's own sister, whom she bore some resemblance to in appearance, with similar Asian features, hair colour and olive complexion.

32. Photo - Baby Doris & father Hedley

As there was an eight-year age difference between the two children, and because Nancy was still so rebellious that Evelyn found her difficult to manage, the arrangement continued, with Nancy spending the majority of her time living at the manse in Ballarat. She wished to remain with her adoptive grandparents and other members of the household where she seemed happiest and most secure. She was old enough to walk to school and as her sister Doris became old enough, she would sometimes spend time staying in Ballarat also. On these visits she attended Golden Point State School with her older sister Nancy accompanying her the short distance from Young Street on foot. It was on one of these occasions that the usual name calling and racist taunts of 'Ching Chong Chinaman' were made against young Doris because she was distinctly Chinese in appearance, in strong contrast with her white-skinned sister. Quick to lose her temper, Nancy immediately retaliated by rushing up to one of the offending boys and she swung a strong punch, hitting him square on the nose! Although he was considerably older and bigger than Nancy, he ran off howling and holding his bloodied nose, crying that he was going to report her to the headmaster. In due course, Nancy was summoned to the office to explain herself before the headmaster and in the presence of the boy's mother who had been sent for. When young Nancy explained the reason for the incident, the mother's reaction was to voice her surprise at how such a small girl could beat up such a big boy, saying 'Well if that's the best he can do, then it serves him right!' Fiery tempered Nancy was thus vindicated and sent back to her classroom without further ado. By this time, Nancy had developed a pride in her Ballarat family and an awareness that the young Chinese descent children in the area were prone to name-calling and teasing because of their Asian appearance. She had developed a protective instinct for her younger, more vulnerable half-caste sister and she felt strongly bound to defend her.

However, in her teenage years, she was able to return to spend more time with her mother, stepfather and young sister Doris in their lovely, double story Victorian-styled, polychromed brick house situated in Barkers Road, Glenferrie. It was directly opposite the Methodist Ladies' College where Doris was enrolled to attend as a new student: a stark contrast to the upbringing and educational opportunities that Nancy had experienced in her own childhood years. Although Nancy did not display any resentment towards young Doris, she continued to withdraw from any intimate relationship possibilities with her mother. Evelyn found she could not exert any control over her daughter's actions, but was constantly met with defiance and indifference. By contrast, Nancy developed a genuine fondness for her good-natured stepfather, Hedley, and behaved altogether differently towards him. He appeared to understand the conflict within her and made no judgements upon her behaviour, unlike her mother. Thus, Nancy saw herself as bonded to the Chinese family far more than in her previous circumstance as an illegitimate white child with unknown Irish parentage and without a father. She felt the need to belong, and this was the choice she made.

Meanwhile in the intervening years, what about Joseph, the eldest son?

33. Photo of Joseph Tong Wai (enlargement from certificate)

In many respects, Joseph was the misfit in the family. Unlike his half siblings, Joseph was not born in this land, and with a thirteen year age gap, he did not possess the same sense of belonging that his step brothers and sisters shared for this country. His early memories and different experiences of village life in China prevented him from bonding in the same way with his family, despite their efforts to include him. The White Australia Policy was so broadly supported by the white majority of the community, that he experienced a lingering sense of isolation and restlessness. Joe was not well educated and advantaged with easy employment prospects like his younger siblings, but faced with a lifetime of very hard physical work and long hours. When the family relocated from Little Bendigo to Golden Point, Joseph did not wish to be a burden, so he decided to try earning a living by hiring a horse and cart and for a short time he tried his luck as a hawker of clothing apparel around the Ballarat district. However, it was not long before he removed himself from Ballarat, as he claimed that his asthma attacks influenced him to seek a change in climate. For a short while he worked as a cobbler's apprentice in Queanbeyan, New South Wales. Finally, at the age of twenty-three years, he decided to return home to China on board the ship *Tsinan* bound for Hong Kong to see if he could reconnect with his relatives in the home village of Wang Tung. At this time, it was after the overthrow of the Qing dynasty. For some reason, possibly the realisation that he could no longer adjust to the life he had left so long ago, he chose not to settle in the village, but returned to Hong Kong where he gained employment in a hotel owned by a Mr Beaurepaire. He was the father of Frank Beaurepaire, who held a reputation at that time as a notable Australian swimmer, later on to become the Lord Mayor of Melbourne. Aided by the fact that he had lived in Australia and spoke some English language, Joseph was employed to escort visiting Europeans between their ship and the hotel. Perhaps realising that he felt no genuine sense of belonging in either country, eventually he decided he would be better placed to establish a decent and more secure life back in Australia where his immediate family was. He was unable to return immediately and was forced to wait out the term of the 1914-18 war when he returned immediately afterwards. Following a visit to see his parents in Ballarat, he decided to settle in Sydney, New South Wales where the climate seemed better suited to his health and because he had no particular wish to remain in Ballarat.

It was here that he found work at the Sydney markets, and after gaining experience in the grocery business, he saved hard to set up his own grocery business in William Street, Paddington. Eventually, with a lot of hard work he gained enough success and prosperity to propose marriage to one of his regular customers who helped him sometimes in the shop. She was Irene Mary Hickey, who was of Irish-European descent. Despite strong racial prejudice and opposition against the marriage by Irene's parents who were devout Irish Catholics and vehemently disliked the idea of her marrying a Chinese, the couple were married on 11th January 1922. They produced three young children: a girl they named Gladys, born 19th September 1925, followed by two boys, Stephen on 31st January 1928 and Michael on 26th January 1933. Sadly, the children became orphaned with the early death of their mother Irene in December 1934. Joe was distraught at losing his wife and without the offer of any sympathy or support from Irene's family nearby, he felt he was unable to care for the two youngest boys and continue his grocery business; so once again John and Mary Tong Way were called upon to come to the rescue.

At their bidding, in 1935 Joe took the two young boys to Ballarat by train to live with their grandparents while Gladys, the eldest and only daughter, remained in Sydney to assist him in the business. It was considered that subsequently the boys would attend Ballarat schools where they could gain a useful education. Michael, the youngest child, was just a baby at only twenty-two months old and thus it was a huge undertaking for the Tong Way couple who were not young and could have anticipated that the years ahead would be easier and less demanding of their time and effort. Having already undertaken the continued care and upbringing of Nancy, and with the prospect of caring for the extra two grandsons in their old age, they could have been forgiven for refusing. However, they saw it as a necessary part of their Christian faith to care for those less fortunate, particularly when it was members of their own family and with the understanding that life circumstances for Joseph had not been easy. Hence, they accepted this extra burden without complaint. The main burden of care fell to Mary to manage the everyday needs of her grandsons without any thought of herself, but almost inevitably, it was not long before tragedy followed the family's fortunes once more.

In 1941 Mary, with a weak heart and completely worn out from the extra demands she had placed upon her strength, suddenly succumbed to heart failure; she experienced an incredible physical weakness which resulted in her being totally bedridden and needing constant care. Their only surviving daughter, Doris, was then teaching at a school in Castlemaine, but over a six-week period she travelled to Ballarat each weekend to take turns at caring for her ailing mother along with my mother, Nancy, Hedley's adopted daughter. On hearing the news, Nancy had immediately left her employment at the Monte Park Mental Hospital, and she came up from Melbourne by train to take on the care of her adored grandmother during the weekdays. At this stage, Nancy had acquired some early nursing experience which enabled her to care devotedly for dear Mary. The doctor seemed unable to do more than recommend complete bed rest and he claimed that it was then 'in the hands of the Lord'. Bedridden, Mary lingered on for many weeks, but it was evident to all in the household that she was losing her grip on life. John Tong Way managed to employ a housekeeper named Miss Leach to do the family washing and also the house cleaning one day each week. Alas, it was a shame that help of this nature was not considered necessary to lighten the workload for poor Mary much more beforehand.

Young Michael was then attending school close by at Golden Point State School and his elder brother Stephen went to Ballarat High School, following in the footsteps of his uncles Sam, Hedley, Kenneth and Aunt Doris, who had been students there some years before. It was a distressing time for the entire household and the children were very subdued around the house, greatly affected by the seriousness of their grandmother's illness. As Mary became visibly weaker each day and her strength had ebbed away, in a weak voice she struggled to say her final goodbyes to each member of the family several hours before she closed her eyes for the last time. Quite unexpectedly that night, John had awoken suddenly and visited her room to sit with her during the early hours after midnight, possibly prompted by his extreme anxiety and a premonition of her death. Doris was there by Mary's bedside, and she woke Nancy to let her know that her grandmother's death was imminent. 'Come quickly, Nancy, I think she is passing away!' Only the day before when young Michael was taken in to visit his beloved grandmother with his older brother Stephen for the last time, he was able to speak with her, later recalling those final, calm and reassuring words she whispered to him, that 'death is just a long sleep'. He has never forgotten that special moment.

With the effects of the Second World War in 1941, and following the death of their grandmother, for a short time the two children were returned to live with their father, Joseph, who had sold his business and relocated from Sydney to East Melbourne. With frugal living he had accumulated enough money to live off his investments and retire in 1938 when he bought a house at 49 Gipps Street. However, the children did not remain with him for very long. It was generally considered that all city children would be safer during the war if sent to live in the country, so the boys were returned to Grandma and Grandpa Tong Way at the manse in Ballarat. Gladys, the eldest, remained in Melbourne to help her father until she met and married

Gordon Nam who was also Chinese, at the very young age of only seventeen years. Joseph had not been born in Australia, unlike his younger siblings in the Tong Way family; hence, he was classified as an alien. This meant that he suffered the indignity of being forced by law to apply for and carry the identification of an Alien's Certificate on his person at all times for the remaining years of the White Australia Policy and almost for the rest of his life.

34. Joseph's Alien Certificate

In this respect, it was difficult to have a strong sense of belonging to the country which accepted his half-brothers and -sisters, but singled him out, due to the circumstances of his birth. Sadly, he was condemned to be permanently considered a non-citizen and therefore he remained in the eyes of officialdom an outsider until the day he died in 1957.

THIRD-GENERATION
CHINESE-AUSTRALIAN
CITIZENS

Following WW1, Sam's career in teaching flourished, driven by his ambition to get on and win the admiration and respect of both his colleagues and the acceptance of the wider community. He achieved this success professionally, but also by committing himself to being fully assimilated into every facet of community life as a worthy Australian citizen. Early on, he recognised that there were more opportunities for early promotion by staying on the roll in the primary school system than in secondary teaching, so he applied for positions which would provide him with the chance for early promotion and upward mobility. Having graduated with a BA degree in 1921 he was well qualified and decided that he preferred to teach in country positions rather than the bigger metropolitan schools. As a qualified teaching graduate, he was first sent to Yarram in 1921 until 1928 and immersed himself fully into the social and sporting life of the town. He played cricket, bowls, golf and tennis and he recalled that the students all nicknamed him affectionately as 'Tongy' at that time. He was on the board of management at the Presbyterian Church, on the committee of the RSL and he also joined the Masonic Lodge. Furthermore, he found that being able to play the piano and organ was an added advantage which made him many country friends. He considered that 'being a headmaster brought you in touch with the community'.

He then moved to Red Cliffs East where he met and became attracted to a young teacher of European descent named Emily Violet Wilkinson, commonly known as 'Vi'. They were married at the Ringwood Presbyterian Church during 1930 and he moved on to teach at Woori Yallock in 1931, followed by Jeparit where he became president of the RSL and joined the Lodge there. He gained promotion to Merbein in 1937 where he remained for another ten years. During this time, in 1939 he established the School Library funded by donations from the Fruit Growers Association and the Australian Natives Association: they presented him with a Life Membership (see image 28), a document he was extremely proud of as an acknowledgement of one of his significant achievements.

35. Photo of Sam as Principal

Sam is remembered favourably by former student Jess Walter from Ballarat for his strong sense of duty and the good deed he and his wife Vi extended to her family. This came about when she was a new student to the Merbein school, due to the recent appointment of her father to a teaching position there. She related how her father was unexpectedly stricken with a severe heart attack and transported immediately to a hospital in Melbourne. Because his wife could not drive, she accompanied him for the several weeks' duration he spent in hospital, leaving Jess and her younger brother in the care of Mr and Mrs Tongway until his recovery. In this respect, Sam demonstrated the strong sense of Christian charity and responsibility towards those under his care in a similar fashion to the pastoral care given by his father, Reverend Tong Way, to his Chinese countrymen.

Prior to his marriage, Sam had visited his family in Ballarat every term holidays, but he now visited only once a year, severing the closer family connection he had maintained previously. According to other members in the Tong Way family, he was increasingly influenced by his wife who seemed uncomfortable with him associating too closely with his 'Chineseness'. Undoubtedly, in practical terms, Vi considered that it would hold him back professionally and limit his opportunities for success in the eyes of WASP society. Sam's parents, particularly his father, were distressed by this distancing and John Tong Way made a telling remark which conveyed his disappointment at the time. 'Sam like you take the eye out of the potato …' However, this was the cultural divide created by many Chinese-Australians as the price of their acceptability and success in a European society. On one of the rare, special occasions when Sam and his wife, plus their young son, David, and daughter, Marjorie, were visiting in Young Street, Ballarat, Vi requested that she and the children would not join the rest of the family during the meal. John had cooked the traditional Chinese dishes for this occasion, all set out in porcelain serving bowls centrally placed on the large wooden dining table from which each member would help themselves in turn, with smaller individual bowls and using their chopsticks. Vi and the children ate their meal separately in an adjoining room, possibly because she was not comfortable for her children to be exposed to this alien tradition. Young Nancy was still living with her grandparents at this time and, many years later, she related this incident to me because she said at the time it upset her and she could not understand why this was necessary. She claimed that, sadly, the two children did not really get to know her and her sister, Doris, as cousins on the rare occasions whenever they came in contact with each other. It appeared to her that Sam was prepared to distance himself and his family as the price of overcoming anti-Chinese prejudice and thus maintaining respectable norms and community expectations He was proud of his 'Australian-ness' and he felt justifiably proud of his many achievements.

36. Rare family group photo (Hedley, back row, 2nd row L-R Evelyn & Ken, 3rd row L-R Vi, Sam & Nancy with baby Doris & Aunt Doris)

In 1948 Sam and Vi moved to Bendigo where he had gained a position teaching at the Violet Street State School. They lived in the school residence until 1953 when he purchased the home at Kangaroo Flat that they were to spend the rest of their lives in. Following his lifelong leadership and participation in community organisations, he soon became the President of Rotary and continued to play bowls. As Rotary President, he prided himself for his promotion of 'Internationalism' by bringing Asian students and visitors to Bendigo. He had developed the progressive idea of bringing the first exchange students from overseas in exchange for the reciprocal visitation of Bendigo students. In 1982 he retired from Rotary and after fifty years of membership in the Free Masons he ceased his involvement. He was visibly proud of the fact in later years that he had been a member of the RSL Senior Citizens for sixty years, was still actively playing bowls and golf, and had been a member of the RACV for fifty-nine years also. He showed me an article he had kept that appeared in the *Bendigo Advertiser*, acknowledging that he was the longest serving member of the Victorian Teachers' Union. Altogether he saw his lifetime achievements as being proof that he was an accepted and respected member of the establishment and a proud elder citizen of Australia.

37. Photo of Sam at bowls

Sadly, he had become estranged from his brother, Hedley, many years before and they had discontinued all contact. Hedley still held his secure position with the Postal Department and gained promotion, possibly aided by the fact that he had always been gifted in mathematics. He remained an entirely different personality to his brother, Sam; less formal and more casual with his acquaintanceships and of course he was still known to have the occasional fling by betting on the horses. It was in conversation with Sam on one of my visits to see him in later years that he still described his brother, disapprovingly, as always 'mixing with a racing crowd'. After the First World War, the brothers had lived together in East Melbourne for a short time before Hedley then resigned from the public service. He left to take up the Soldier Settlement block at Lake Goldsmith near Beaufort and Sam left for a teaching position at Yarram.

During the Christmas holidays much later on, Sam helped him with the fencing and taking off the potato crop at his second farming venture situated at Dean. This period created the beginning of the seemingly irreparable rift between the two brothers. Sam claimed that he lost his wartime gratuity money by helping Hedley and investing it in the farm. He recalled that the land was infested with blackberries: despite the hard labour they endured, plus the fact that both brothers had initially put their entire gratuities into Hedley's farm, it was not a viable proposition for such novices. Also, Sam claimed that because Hedley's lungs had been affected by gas from his war experiences, he should have accepted from his earlier failed attempt at Lake Goldsmith that he was not physically suited to farming. However, Hedley ended up selling the property at a loss and he re-entered the Postal Department on the Returned Servicemen's Preference scheme. This soured the relationship, as Sam claimed that Hedley owed him, and his money was never repaid. He disapproved of the company his brother kept and, knowing that his brother liked to 'have a bit of a fling', he once again said of Hedley in later years, 'Still the same crowd of people, Australians racing'. Hedley's marriage to Evelyn Scanlon was another problem, because Sam was a pillar of respectability and his brother's choice would have come into question as a poor decision.

From that point they shared little in common and their paths led in entirely different directions. Unfortunately, with the eventual breakup of his marriage to Evelyn on the tragic loss of their daughter, Doris, in 1950, Hedley faced the harshest judgement from his father in particular. John Tong Way saw his action of forsaking his marital responsibilities and seeking a divorce to marry Gladys, his new partner in Adelaide, as an unforgivable sin. Therefore, he resolutely refused to have any further contact with Hedley until the day he died. Consequently, Hedley became totally ostracised by the rest of the family, who appeared to have become similarly influenced in their thinking.

Doris, the only surviving daughter had also chosen the teaching profession because it offered her as an unmarried spinster a position of security and respectability.

38. Photo of Doris

She had excelled at school equally with her older brothers and paved her way with scholarships to the point where, in 1920, at the age of 22 years, she entered Teacher's College in Gratton Street, Carlton. She had previously become engaged to a young Ballarat man of European descent who was her Ballarat sweetheart before the war years. When WW1 was declared, he enlisted in the AIF, but due to the disapproval and racial prejudice of his parents against the marriage, their engagement was broken off before he departed for war service overseas. Sadly, he was killed in action and never returned; it was then she determined that she would never marry. Prior to winning the scholarship, in 1918 she joined the Education Department and began as a junior teacher at the Ballarat Orphanage school. Over the following forty-four years, she remained a spinster, living and teaching at a variety of schools. She stayed for an extended period of thirteen years in the Victorian countryside at Newstead State School where, on a recent visit to the town, I was reminded that she had been a much-loved member of staff and the community. She was extremely innovative and creative, working on beautifully artistic collages made up with the silver and gold sweet-wrappings she encouraged the students to collect for her. From an early age, Doris had displayed considerable artistic talent, and, during her career, her artistic skills were evident from her pencil and ink drawings as well as her delicate silver-paper framed collage figures of fairies and flowers. As a child, I remember being fascinated to watch the painstaking care she took in creating these delicate works. The school donated some of these treasures to the local Newstead Museum which remain in their extensive collection today.

39. Doris' artwork

Earlier in her career at Newstead State School as the Infant mistress, she was also responsible for the sewing classes. Whilst there, she boarded locally in the home of the headmaster, Mr Frederick Walter Ellis, who remained in the school from 1915 until his retirement in 1933. He spoke highly of this tiny-but-formidable and capable Miss

Tong Way as a greatly valued teacher and member of the school community. Although diminutive in size, her students recognised that she would brook no nonsense and she expected hard work from all of them as she equally demonstrated herself! Thus, after thirteen rewarding years of teaching in rural Newstead, she was given a huge send-off by the school community and presented with a special writing desk which she treasured always.

40. Doris at writing desk

according to the car sticker philosophy old teachers never die, they simply lose their class. It is interesting to ponder that many do attain a certain immortality in that their influence reaches down through many years — perhaps generations.

At the age of six I began school in our small country town and was immediately taken in hand by our Chinese infants' teacher. Short, fat and totally unflappable, she sat enthroned before us, in complete command of "babies", first and second classes — probably twenty to thirty of us.

To sit in Miss Tongway's reading class was to achieve membership of an exclusive group of those who had learnt all their sounds by much monotonous chanting under the smug tutelage of a monitor. Her dark eyes rested on us as we read aloud

I know now that she was a teacher of truly outstanding ability.

Miss Tongway left Newstead for Castlemaine. She retired there Later and died during 1980's. A.M.C.

41. Excerpt letter former pupil

She continued her teaching career in a number of schools, and later on, in 1950, when she gained a promotion to Castlemaine North State School as a grade teacher and infant mistress, she purchased her own home at 32 Myring Street Castlemaine. It is here she lived before and after her retirement in 1962. She was also a keen philatelist and botanist. During her retirement, of great interest to her was the Kaweka Sanctuary situated in the rear bushland to her home, where she collected native wildflowers. From these she utilised her talents by making many card and flower arrangements which she sold and donated the proceeds to the Sanctuary and the Rice Bowl Appeal. As an acknowledgement of her efforts, one of the tracks in the Sanctuary is named after her as The Tongway Walk. She used to call her donations her 'apron money'.

In the twilight years of John Tong Way's working life, it was recognised that he was to be the last of the superintendent missioners to the Chinese in Ballarat. After the death of his wife, Mary, he remained at Young Street in the old manse a further eight years with his youngest grandson, Michael, until 1949, when at eighty-seven years, John was experiencing failing health. He decided that, with only three left in his remnant congregation and no prospect of more Chinese members, he would retire and move with Michael to live with his father, Joseph, in East Melbourne. Michael had been attending Ballarat High School at this time, but his elder brother Stephen had already departed for further studies in Melbourne. Their elder sister, Gladys, had already married Gordon Nam, of Chinese descent, and they had settled into family life in a terrace-styled house in central East Melbourne, later to celebrate the births of their two daughters, Lynette and Maureen. Doris took over the care of her elderly father in 1956 after he had spent the previous seven years with Joe, her half-brother and her father's eldest son. Joe sadly predeceased his father and died of stomach cancer in 1957. In his final twilight years, John Tong Way was content to potter about in the vegetable garden at his daughter's Castlemaine property, with ongoing father-daughter differences of opinion about whether to replace her precious flower garden with what he regarded as a more productive vegetable garden.

After John Tong Way's death in 1960 at 99 years of age, the family recalled that John had always regarded his age as 100 years, because in China, age included one's life from the time of conception and not from birth. Regardless, he had led a remarkable life. His grandson Michael described the day of his burial: 'It was a brilliantly sunny and very warm Wednesday, on the 21st December 1960, that saw John Tong Way returned for the last time to his beloved Ballarat, to his final resting place'. On the side of his grave is carved the fitting words in tribute to his unceasing and tireless missionary work among his fellow countrymen; the inscription simply reads:

'BLESSED ARE THEY WHO DIE IN THE LORD'

42. Photo of John Tong Way's grave

Doris remained living alone in Castlemaine until mid-1980 when she was diagnosed with cancer. For the remainder of her days, she lived in a granny flat adjoining the home of her devoted nephew Michael Way, his wife Wendy and their family at Mt. Waverley until her death on 20th July 1981. She was buried in the family grave alongside her parents at the Ballarat New Cemetery according to her wishes, whereas Michael's father Joseph, still solitary, was buried in a separate grave in the Melbourne Cemetery.

THE END OF AN ERA

Sadly, with the retirement of John Tong Way, in 1949 the Presbyterian Church hierarchy had decided to remove the simple wooden church building from its location at number 6 Young Street to perform a new function in Ballarat North, where the building might be useful for a new, white congregation. For a lifetime of dedicated work among his Chinese countrymen 'winning souls' and on behalf of the Presbyterian church, the only symbol of acknowledgement and recognition for all this faithful service was a small bronze plaque which was attached to an exterior wall by the entrance of the Chinese Mission Church. It acknowledged his life's work on behalf of the Chinese congregation, but over time, it seems it was not considered worthy of collection and preservation as a historical archive. All of my attempts to locate it in Ballarat have failed and consequently it appears to have been lost to history. Sadly, so little was the church recognised as a unique remnant of Ballarat's Chinese Australian heritage, that the plaque was removed along with the building and, despite local rumour that it was in the care of the Ballarat Historical Society collection, it has never been located. Perhaps this fact alone is a testament to the disinterest and silence which, until recently, has been maintained towards the contribution the Chinese made to the growth and development of Ballarat, both during and since the goldrush era; a period in which Reverend John Tong Way and his family were a significant, contributing part.

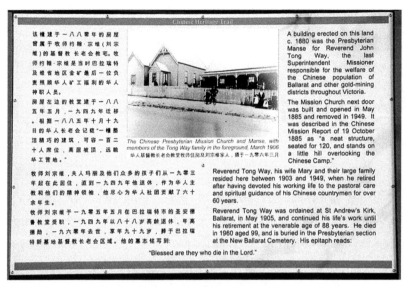

The Chinese Presbyterian Mission Church and Manse, with members of the Tong Way family in the foreground, March 1906
华人基督教长老会教堂牧师住房及刘宗唯家人，摄于一九零六年三月

该幢建于一八八零年的房屋曾属于牧师约翰·宗唯（刘宗唯）的基督教长老会教宅。牧师约翰·宗唯是当时巴拉瑞特及维省地区金矿最后一位负责照顾华人矿工福利的华人神职人员。

房屋在边的教堂建于一八八五年五月，一九四九年拆移。根据一八八五年十月十九日的华人长老会记载"一幢整洁精巧的建筑，可容一百二十人席位，高居坡顶，远眺华工营地。"

牧师刘宗唯，夫人玛丽及他们众多的孩子们从一九零三年起在此居住，直到一九四九年他退休，作为华人主教和他们的精神领袖，他尽心为华人社团贡献了六十余年生。

牧师刘宗唯于一九零五年五月在巴拉瑞特市的圣安德鲁教堂受职，一九四九年以八十八岁高龄退休，年高德劭，一九六零年去世，享年九十九岁，葬于巴拉瑞特新墓地基督教长老会区域。他的墓志铭写到：

A building erected on this land c. 1880 was the Presbyterian Manse for Reverend John Tong Way, the last Superintendent Missioner responsible for the welfare of the Chinese population of Ballarat and other gold-mining districts throughout Victoria.

The Mission Church next door was built and opened in May 1885 and removed in 1949. It was described in the Chinese Mission Report of 19 October 1885 as "a neat structure, seated for 120, and stands on a little hill overlooking the Chinese Camp."

Reverend Tong Way, his wife Mary and their large family resided here between 1903 and 1949, when he retired after having devoted his working life to the pastoral care and spiritual guidance of his Chinese countrymen for over 60 years.

Reverend Tong Way was ordained at St Andrew's Kirk, Ballarat, in May 1905, and continued his life's work until his retirement at the venerable age of 88 years. He died in 1960 aged 99, and is buried in the Presbyterian section at the New Ballarat Cemetery. His epitaph reads:

"Blessed are they who die in the Lord."

43. Photo of sign at 6 Young St

However, change does eventually happen! More recently, with co-operation from the Ballarat City Council and support from close local neighbours, I have succeeded in getting the side lane renamed Tong Way Place. In addition, an information plaque erected in front of the former manse building still standing at number 6 Young Street. Furthermore, on Sunday 6th September 2015, a new memorial was erected on the reserve at the corner of Main Road and Barkly Street to finally acknowledge the contribution the Chinese have made to the history and heritage of Ballarat. Michael Way, grandson of Reverend John Tong Way, proudly attended the unveiling of the monument that day to represent the family.

44. Michael Way & new monument

Nancy's Own Story

My name is Nancy Way, and the story I have to tell about my childhood is a most unusual one for the time. I was a white child of Anglo-Irish descent who once lived at number 6 Young Street, Ballarat East, in the household of my adoptive Chinese grandparents, Reverend John and Mrs Mary Tong Way, whom I adored more than my own absent parents. Here, I was accepted and included in the daily routine amongst 'family' along with uncles Ken and Gordon; and of course, I became quite at home with all other representatives of the local Chinese congregation who visited the little wooden Mission Church next door to the Presbyterian Manse where we lived.

At six and a half years of age I attended the Golden Point State School nearby, and later learned to help my Chinese grandfather by playing the organ in the church each Sunday to accompany the rather tuneless intonations of the all-male Chinese congregation. In those days, they were mostly the elderly Chinese market gardeners from Humffray Street South and the nearby White Flat, close by to the old, red brick woollen mill where they had their market gardens and grew their vegetables. They could easily be identified pulling their hand carts around the streets daily, stacked with fresh produce grown from the rich river soils of their gardens; or on Sundays, shuffling along in single file, uphill towards the Chinese Mission Church in Young Street with their hands always folded behind their backs. They appeared to travel this way as a residue of their quaint and customary lifelong habits that they brought with them from their homeland. As a child, I was fascinated with their quaint appearance and their different ways. At this time of my life I began to consider myself to be one of the Chinese also, having scant consciousness that any physical difference mattered or even attracted the slightest attention; unaware of a raised eyebrow or two. All that counted was, I could now claim that I had a father and besides a mother I had a proper family, with grandparents and a home I belonged to.

At six years of age, I had been rescued from the orphanage in which my mother had placed me two years before as an illegitimate, fatherless four-year-old of unknown Irish descent. My time at the orphanage had been a traumatic experience and, as far as I was concerned, Hedley Tong Way, the man who became my new father, was my saviour! My rescue happened when he began courting my mother, Evelyn Maria Scanlon, and he visited the Blackburn orphanage with her one Sunday afternoon on her day off from her live-in workplace at Kew, where she was a housemaid and part time child-career for a wealthy family; a situation for me that held a certain irony under the circumstances. I was crying at the time and alone in the dormitory where I had been left as a punishment because I had become a constant bed-wetter.

The orphanage was in a large, two story, brick building that contained lengthy rooms divided into two rows, with beds either side. When they first entered the room, I remember meeting Hedley as a kind stranger with yellowish skin and funny eyes who appeared quite shocked to see I was not being properly looked after and that I was sick, miserable, and neglected. I had a very high temperature and the constant punishment I received for wetting the bed meant that the diet of bread and water I was often given as punishment had caused me to become very thin and under-nourished. He immediately took it upon himself to summon a doctor to see me that afternoon. It was after this that he decided to ask my mother to marry him. He plucked up the courage and said that if my mother agreed to accept his proposal, he would adopt me as well: a small, sickly, blue-eyed, illegitimate Irish waif.

I later found out that they had met on an arranged date organised by a friend named Alf who happened to be married to Evelyn's older sister, Mary. They had taken pity on him when Hedley told them that he was without a girlfriend because he looked Chinese; he felt rejected by the fairer sex and he was feeling very lonely. When he finally met my mother, he was aware that she was one of the few eligible females who were either brave or desperate enough to marry a full-blooded Australian Chinese. When he plucked up the courage to ask her to marry him and offered to make a home for me as well, my mother did not hesitate before she gave her answer: 'Yes, Hedley I will!' At the time, my mother was not thinking of the likelihood that she may be rejected by her family because of this. She simply desired a life of respectability and security; it was the opportunity to have a home and a good provider for the both of us to have a decent life. Her decision had unforeseen consequences in the oncoming years however, because my mother experienced a great deal of mingled resentment and jealousy from her sisters who demonstrated their feelings with ill-disguised racism. Apart from expressing their dislike of Hedley's Asian ancestry, their animosity was strengthened because my mother had married well above them into an educated, professionally respectable and successful family that were able to afford a nice home despite their Chinese-ness.

The outcome of her decision to marry Hedley and remove me from the orphanage also had other unforeseen consequences for my mother. After we were reunited with each other as mother and daughter, she discovered that we had a problem: the long separation from each other and the physical and emotional deprivations I had suffered during my time in the orphanage meant that, from the outset of their marriage, I behaved coldly and rather resentfully towards her. I blamed her for my abandonment in the orphanage. My silent moods created a problem for them both and of course, I became a bit of a handful to inherit overnight at the beginning of their life as a newly wedded couple. My withdrawal and rejection of my mother was placing a strain on their relationship, and they despaired of what to do with me. It was mainly my mother I punished, because Hedley was my new, kind father and I liked him. Eventually, Hedley decided to visit his parents in Ballarat, and he spoke with them about their dilemma and the difficulties they were having in helping me to settle in, wondering if they could help in some way. Finally, it was decided that I would adjust better if I was taken to Ballarat on a visit to meet my new adoptive grandparents, Reverend John and Mary Tong Way.

When I met them at first, I was curious and did not know what to expect; the Reverend was very tall and slightly stooped, with greying hair and wearing a dark suit with the rounded collar of a minister. He bowed and shook my hand to greet me in a very formal way, but on meeting my grandma I took a liking almost straight away to this quaint, tiny, little, smooth-faced lady with the beaming smile and a funny sing-song way of speaking. She took me to a room behind the kitchen where there was a single bed covered by a patchwork quilt and a simple wooden dresser alongside a wooden chair. 'You our granddaughter now. You please come stay with us a while?' she asked me. I was curious about this new situation, so I nodded my agreement to her kindly, smiling face.

We returned to the kitchen where she had prepared some watery-looking chicken soup for our lunch, with a few strange vegetables floating on the surface. I had been told by Hedley that I was to get to know my new grandparents and stay with them in Ballarat East for a holiday period at the manse until things became more settled in Melbourne. At that stage, I was quite happy for the time being to satisfy my curiosity and get to know them, plus meet the other members of the household who were to be my new grown-up uncles, Gordon and Ken. I had also heard quite a lot about their older sister, Aunt Doris, who was away teaching at a school in the country, but often came to visit her parents and brothers on weekends. Hedley had told me that she was very clever at making things and could draw beautiful pictures which she might show me. He sounded very proud of his only sister and, at the time, I did not know that years ago he had another younger sister called Gladys who was also very clever. He told me that she was much loved amongst the family, her schoolteachers and friends, as well as the non-Chinese community from St John's Presbyterian Church where she attended regularly on Sundays. Tragically and inexplicably, she had died suddenly at only seventeen years of age without hardly any warning. She was mourned greatly by all who knew her, but especially Grandma. I later realised that Grandma never fully recovered from the terrible shock of this unexpected loss, because she would tremble and cry if Gladys was ever mentioned.

Strangely, although I must have stood out like a sore toe, I adjusted well to my new situation, holding no reservations towards my ageing and kindly Chinese grandparents as I grew to love them dearly. Gradually I felt more settled and secure with my world, and I remember displaying none of the earlier moods and refusal to co-operate that I had demonstrated towards my parents in Melbourne. I developed a genuine affection for my strange, tiny grandma with her unusual Asian features and the funny, shuffling walk she always had in her slippered feet. She smiled and explained to me in her strange sing-song voice that, 'You just like me', because when she was a baby in China, her parents had also left her at an orphanage. This was because she was a girl baby and they were very poor rice farmers. Boy babies were considered far more valuable to keep at home and later on they would hope to marry a son into a family that could afford to pay them a good dowry for their daughter. This was the tradition back in her village in China, she told me. 'Poor families not afford to keep daughters', she said. The problem was that as a baby, before she was left at the orphanage in Hong Kong, her feet had been bound very tightly, because this was a valued Chinese custom. It was considered to be an advantage for females to have very tiny feet so they would be more likely to appear dainty and attractive and it would help their chances to marry well when they grew older. What finally prompted her parents to give up their daughter is left to our guesswork, but their extreme poverty was most likely the cause. It gave us an added affinity with each other, strengthened by this shared experience we had from our childhood circumstances.

However, the Lutheran nuns at the Bethesda Orphanage in Hong Kong where she was raised considered foot binding to be a terrible, heathen practice and they removed the tight bindings in the hope that any damage could be avoided. Unfortunately, it was too late and much damage had been done. The bones in her toes and feet had been bent back so severely that they were now broken and deformed, so they could never be mended and made normal again. I could not bear to look at them and I realised that this was the main reason that my little grandmother never walked beyond the house and garden. Her only outings were on the rare occasions when she was accompanied by me or another family member to choose a birthday present, or on a special occasion such as Christmas. She would don her strong black ankle boots and painstakingly totter along, holding onto my arm or accompanied by other members of the family. These were my new cousins, Stephen and Michael, who had come to stay also. They were the sons of Uncle Joe, the eldest son of my grandfather who was born in China to my grandfather's first wife who died. It was explained to me that Joe came to join his father here on the goldfields of Ballarat in 1892 at eleven years of age and that he was the half-brother to my grandfather Hedley and his siblings. Uncle Joe had a grocery store in Sydney and his wife died when Michael was just a baby. Because his in-laws were strict Irish Catholics, they never accepted their daughter's marriage to a Chinese and offered Joseph no help with his three young, motherless children. My goodhearted grandparents then came to their rescue as they did for me. Gladys, the eldest, stayed to help her father in Sydney, whilst my grandparents, John and Mary, took in their two motherless grandsons to care for as well as me. This must have been such a strain for Grandma to have all this extra work, but she never complained, and although we loved her, we did not really understand the sacrifice she was making or the heavy toll it took on her energies and health to look after us.

A New Life Begins

In 1930, to my surprise I was told I had a half-Chinese baby sister who was named Doris Winifred after my aunt Doris the schoolteacher.

I did not meet my baby sister for a while because, apart from occasional visits, I did not return permanently to live with my parents in Melbourne but continued to remain mostly in Ballarat where I was happy and settled. She was a beautiful child, and she had the Asian features of her father, Hedley, with the dark eyes and complexion, plus the rich black hair of her exotic ancestry. The distance of eight years between my half-sister and I meant that I did not particularly wish to be back home with a baby sister, and it gave my parents time to be new parents without having to worry about me. Although I was very much a white child in appearance, I felt that I had a family here in Ballarat who had genuinely welcomed me, and it was where I felt a sense of belonging. Therefore, I was happy to continue staying in the home of Reverend John Tong Way and be placed in the loving care of his

Chinese wife, my grandma, Mary. My visit ultimately extended into years instead of months, because it became my happy place where I felt loved and secure, and it was where I wanted to be. Grandma Tong Way was a remarkable woman and proved to be the only one who could really manage me. I enjoyed to just be at home with her when I was not attending school and I loved to help her with the chores as she patiently taught me so much.

45. Photo of Baby Doris with Evelyn

The experience of living as a white child in a Chinese community during the 1930s was a unique one, which gave me an understanding of what it was like to be born Chinese. Seen through my eyes, I could relate to the cruelty of the taunts and subsequent brawls endured by the children of Chinese descent due to racist attitudes at school amongst the pupils and, quite often, ignored by the teachers. When young Doris came to visit and stay with me at Golden Point on one particular occasion, I decided to take her with me to school for the day. Unfortunately, an incident occurred that aroused my fierce Irish temper, which was prone to happen occasionally. I had already seen the teasing meted out towards some Chinese because of the visible differences in their appearance. Where Doris and I were concerned, we certainly did not look like sisters, as we were a contrasting pair. I was blue-eyed, short and slightly built, with western features, white skin and light brown hair. Young Doris was visibly of Chinese descent, with her thick, long plaits of straight, jet-black hair, olive skin and Asian features, so that when the taunts of 'Ching Chong Chinaman' towards my young sister rang out sharply in my ears, I was immediately enraged and provoked into a fist fight with one of the bigger bullies who was calling out the loudest. I stopped the bicycle and confronted this bully of a boy; although he was much bigger than me, my time in the orphanage had given me plenty of experience at looking after myself, much to the surprise of the recipients! I ran forward and to his surprise, I swung a hard punch straight at his big, ugly nose and caused it to bleed. Of course, he ran off bawling his eyes out, along with his cowardly friends, and made such a fuss that I was called into the headmaster's office to explain myself. The mother was contacted and next day I was hauled over the coals once more to make an apology. I walked into the office, trying to disguise how nervous I felt, but when she saw me, she seemed surprised and commented on how small I was. She said to the headmaster, 'Well if he can let a small girl like her get the better of him in a fight, then he deserves what he got!' With that, she promptly took her leave and I was permitted to return to the classroom without any punishment. After that, word must have been passed around, because there were no further incidents of name calling again when I was with my little sister in the local neighbourhood. Unfortunately for her, Doris had a quiet disposition and was very timid and shy; hence this experience did nothing to improve her self-confidence when in unfamiliar or new situations. I was always regarded as the bossy, fiery-tempered one, but my upbringing was very different to the mollycoddling childhood that my half-sister experienced and it prepared me well for some of the hardships that life dealt me in the years to come.

My time ended up being divided into six-monthly intervals between Melbourne and Ballarat, which meant that I had a very fragmented education, with Golden Point being the only stable school amongst the others that were constantly changing with every house move when staying in Melbourne with my parents. Firstly, I was enrolled at Heidelberg State School when we lived in a house near the Gasworks by the river. At this time, Hedley's sister, Aunty Doris, often came to stay with us. After this, because of the uncertain nature of housing rental and Hedley's different workplaces in the public service, there were frequent moves. At Clifton Hill State School I remember that I contracted both measles and mumps, which were extremely contagious at the time. After that I attended Bentleigh State School, followed by Pascoe Vale State School where my young sister, Doris, was also enrolled for the first year.

46. Photo of young Doris, 1936, L-R, 5th in centre row

The class photo singles her out from the other children because of her Asian features and olive complexion. By this time, I was in the eighth grade. Eventually, I finished my schooling by attending the Girls' Technical School in Barkly Street, Ballarat East, leaving at the earliest stage possible, as I was eager to find a job, earn my own money and become part of the working world. In this respect, I had not absorbed the strong influence of my Chinese grandparents to make higher education my goal. Instead, I left the secure confines of my grandparents' home in the Ballarat manse and returned to live permanently in Melbourne with my parents, Hedley and Evelyn, in Barkers Road. This I justified because of better employment opportunities seeking factory work, and from then on I was expected to contribute financially to the household by paying board once I was earning a wage. In many respects, it was a period of missed opportunities and I lived to regret it throughout my later life.

I reflected upon this earlier time as almost like living two separate lives. When in Ballarat, I was restricted and constrained by the strict household discipline and willingly complied with their expected norms. I attended the morning services with the family at St John's

Presbyterian Church, walking downhill to where it was located in nearby Peel Street.

47. St Johns Presbyterian Church

The afternoons were taken up with attendance at the Chinese Mission church next-door to the manse in Young Street. My reverend grandfather delivered his sermons in Cantonese to the small but regular congregation of elderly Chinese market gardeners who faithfully attended. I will never forget the curious spectacle they created for many of the local onlookers as they slowly mounted the slope towards Young Street in their single files, strangely garbed with their broad straw hats and loose clothing, keen to attend the service he delivered in their own familiar dialect. However, few of them ever converted to Christianity, not as John Tong Way had always hoped. Every year his written report to the church leaders in Melbourne detailed how disappointingly few converts he had made, despite his dedicated service. The ageing Chinese often continued to visit their own wooden joss now in Main Road, but once located in the grounds of the former Chinese camp situated on the slope below the manse in Young Street. They worshipped their ancestors in the traditional customs of their ancient culture, but they also supported John Tong Way with their dual attendance. This was born from a sense of loyalty and obligation for the many kindnesses and pastoral care they received from him as their fellow countryman. After the service each Sunday, they would be invited to the large kitchen of the manse where Mary would offer them tea and refreshments. John would also spend some time in the front room attending to any clerical requirements, such as translating or writing their letters, plus advising them on any concerns they may have had and, on some occasions, even representing them in court. He even organised for a few to have their remains disinterred and their bones eventually shipped back to the Tung Wah society in China for reburial in the village of their birth, thereby undertaking to fulfil their final wish.

At all times, I had willingly helped Mary, my kind, hard-working little grandma, with many of the household chores as if I was her Chinese daughter, but it was in a marked contrast to my time living with my parents in Melbourne. I became even more rebellious and often defied my birth mother, with whom I had continued to develop a dysfunctional relationship, refusing to tell her what I was doing or where I was going, as I resented her belated efforts at parenthood.

However, I had become fond of my adoptive father, Hedley, and treated him differently, because he never interfered in our arguments and continued to treat me kindly, as if he understood my conflict. I boasted to some of my new friends that, 'Away from Ballarat, I am regarded as being a bit of a tomboy'. I was physically quite energetic and fit, so I became interested in sporting activities and joined the Richmond Women's Rowing Club as an early member. It was considered to be not that ladylike and not a very common activity for a female at this time. Because of my size at only 5 feet 2 inches, I became the cox at the head of the row-boat, where they practiced regularly on the Yarra River. Of course, my mother disapproved of my 'tom-boy' interests and complained about my continually defiant behaviour over which she had no control. I was quite fond of my young half-sister, Doris, and felt no resentment towards her, but the considerable gap in our ages and the times we were separated from each other prevented us from building further upon the relationship.

48. Nancy and sister Doris Way

I reserved my resentment for my mother who had abandoned me as a homeless, unloved waif in my eyes. Unlike the uncertainties and misfortunes of my own upbringing, Doris was doted upon by two loving parents from the time of her birth and she was raised in a comfortable and secure home: it was a double-storey, polychromed brick, Victorian house situated opposite the Methodist Ladies' College in Barkers Road, Hawthorn. This was the exclusive private school where Doris was enrolled to complete her education. How different her young life was to mine.

49. Methodists Ladies College

AN UNFORSEEN TURN OF EVENTS

In 1941, when I was almost nineteen, I returned unexpectedly to Ballarat, prompted by the distressing news that Grandma Tong Way was seriously ill. I had known she suffered from a weak heart, but the seriousness of this matter had never completely registered whilst I lived amongst the family. We had all taken her for granted whilst she tended to our needs so willingly and without complaint. After a few jobs doing factory work, I had begun working in the Mont Park Mental Asylum as a nursing aid, but without hesitation I immediately handed in my resignation with the intention of caring for her as long as it was necessary. I felt it was the least I could do in return for all the love and care she had bestowed upon me. I had spent the happiest part of my life with her and wanted to help her recover. It was a shock when I saw her, so weak and inert, lying in bed for the first time I had ever seen her do so during the daytime. She had taken to her bed several days before, according to my aunt Doris, Hedley's sister who had come down from Castlemaine where she was teaching, but because of this she could only come on weekends. We decided that I would nurse Grandma during the weekdays, and Doris would take over on weekends, taking it turn-about for our rest times in between. When I greeted Grandma, she smiled to see me, but it was heartrending to see how weak she was, barely able to lift her hand towards me. The weeks went by and I realised that she was gradually fading away as her strength continued to ebb from her tiny body. I tried to keep up a brave front, but knew that there was little I could do other than attend to her basic nursing needs and show how much I cared for her with my actions. Grandfather Tong Way seemed bewildered and wandered about at a loss to do anything other than pray for her, because this time, his herbal remedies were futile. In a very uncustomary action, he awoke and crept into the bedroom to be with Mary very late one night in the third week of my stay. It was on a night when Aunt Doris was on duty. He just sat, huddled by the bed for many hours, silently praying to himself. He must have had a presentiment of Mary's death being imminent, because she quietly passed away in the early hours of that morning as if in her sleep, without opening her eyes to see him for the last time. Aunt Doris woke me and tearfully told me that she thought she was gone. I was glad of my nursing experience then, as we shared the task of lovingly laying her out and preparing her body for the funeral to come. Each member of the household spent time with her to say their private farewells – even her grandsons. Young

Michael, who was then only six years old, and his older brother, Stephen, who was eleven, were allowed to come and see her for the last time, peacefully at rest. Michael had previously visited her the day before while she was still conscious, when it was realised that she would not recover. In later life he never forgot that special moment when she reassured him that 'Death is just a long sleep and nothing to be afraid of'. Uncle Joe and I stayed on for several days following the funeral to help Grandfather with things and generally give him some support until we felt we could leave him. Some of his many friends and members of the church were at hand to visit and make sure he was coping. Aunt Doris had already returned to her school and, afterwards, I took my leave also, in the sad realisation that it was the end of an era and the passing of a precious person from our lives.

Needless to say, I had grown away from my immediate family emotionally by this stage, and it was time to move on with my adult life. As fortune would determine, it was an incidental, totally by chance meeting at Glenferrie Railway Station with a good looking, dark haired, tall young man called Ronald Lidgerwood that soon changed my focus. We started chatting and he insisted on walking me home, saying, 'It is too late to be walking on your own'. This was despite the fact that Barkers Road was much further to walk to than where he lived at Bowen Street, only half way there! In conversation we discovered that we both enjoyed sport, and it turned out that Ron also loved cycling. From then on, I decided that I would like to get to know him more and, as we both shared an interest in cycling, I decided that I would join the same cycling club that welcomed women members. Needless to say, it was considered by my parents as an unusual sporting activity for young women and most unladylike for me to get involved on a competitive basis. However, I was competitive by nature and saw this as a challenge and an opportunity to make an impression upon Ron, my new interest. I decided to save up all the money I earned from my current factory job and eventually bought an imported, very expensive and extremely lightweight racing bicycle suitably designed for my own small weight and stature. We shared many a road race together and I proved to be quite a tough competitor, even in the mixed road races. I was very proud of this bicycle and described it to my own children in later years when reminiscing about my prowess as a champion rider. I even pointed out the route I regularly took when riding across the bridge over the Yarra River, rain, hail or shine on my way to work in those days. It was my main form of transport and kept me fit at the same time.

Ron and I soon developed a close bond and became soulmates and sweethearts as time passed. It was after the Second World War had begun in 1939, Ron joined the Air Force along with his close friend Dougy McAuley and many of his other mates, who were soon to be shipped off to serve; some were based in Darwin and Ron eventually ended up overseas in New Guinea.

50. RAAF photo of Ron

We decided to get married at a registry office in a civil service ceremony without a great deal of pomp or celebration. After a time spent staying with relatives, we rented an old house in South Yarra. There I was to spend a considerable amount of time as a solitary, lonely newlywed because of Ron's absence at the war. In 1942, in a Prahran hospital I gave birth to a daughter we named Yvonne Joan Lidgerwood. She was given a French name after my favourite aunty, Vonnie, who had been recently taken ill with the dreaded tuberculosis and was not expected to live. I thought it would be nice for her to know her name would be continued in the family. There is a lovely photo of her nursing my half-sister Doris as a baby shortly before she died.

51. Aunty "Vonnie" nursing Doris

Little did I know at the time how profoundly this contagious disease would continue to affect our family in the years to come.

Because of the war, I spent most of the time raising baby Yvonne as a single parent in Ron's absence.

Naturally we were bonded very closely as mother and daughter and, because of this, she was very much the focus of all my attention. At the time, Yvonne was old enough to sleep in a cot, but it became the usual practice for her to get up early in the morning, climb out of the cot in her own bedroom, jump into my bed and snuggle up next to her mummy. Imagine the shock she experienced one morning when as usual, she crept into the bed and found a stranger there asleep beside her mother! Ron had returned on leave the previous evening after Yvonne had been put to bed. For young Yvonne, it was a matter of ownership, and as she climbed up into the bed and saw this man asleep next to her mother, she promptly sat with her wet nappy placed squarely on this intruder's face. How dare he! Of course, Ron reacted very quickly by throwing his arms up and almost falling out of the bed along with his angry young daughter. It made me laugh at the time, but Ron failed to see the funny side at first. Not recognising this person, Yvonne viewed him as an unwelcome stranger in her mother's bed, because she had no memory of him as her father. In many cases, the children who were separated from their fathers by active service in the war effort as Yvonne was, were labelled war babies.

BAD NEWS EVENTUATES

In 1945 I gave birth to our second child, a son we named William Robert after his grandfather on Ron's side of the family. However, I did not really seem to recover fully from the birth and found it hard to engage in motherhood with the enthusiasm that I had felt for the birth of Yvonne. Thus, by the time the baby had reached six months and Yvonne was three years old, I had begun to suffer coughing fits and shortness of breath, with frequent bouts of feverishness and I became quite unwell. This was most unusual, because I had always been extremely fit and active, due to my past sporting activities. In trepidation, I finally consulted a local doctor who proceeded to send me for x-rays and other tests. Imagine my shock and despair when I was given the prognosis that I had contracted tuberculosis and was highly contagious. Furthermore, my baby son was also examined to discover that he had developed a shadow on the lung at only six months of age and must also be hospitalised along with myself. Young Yvonne and my husband Ron, were also x-rayed, but, apart from some scarring tissue in the lungs, the disease had not taken hold. It was considered to be one of the deadliest diseases, and at that stage there was no cure to guarantee any recovery. My thoughts immediately turned to my daughter and son and what was to become of them. I was informed that I would immediately need to make preparations to enter the Heatherton Sanatorium, where I would be kept in permanent quarantine, isolated completely from others to prevent the spread of this feared and very contagious disease.

52. Heatherton Sanitarium

At this stage, my husband, Ron, was at his wit's end with worry and consternation about me and also the worry of how he would be able to care for our young daughter and son in my absence. I remember so well how I felt about telling my parents and friends this devastating news. It did not make me believe there was much hope for my recovery when one of the first things my mother rushed to organise was a formal family photo to be taken at a studio. Everyone was dressed in their Sunday best and lined up in a group which consisted of my immediate family and the sisters of Evelyn either side, with my tiny daughter standing in front of me. Uncannily, young Yvonne seemed instinctively to read the gloomy mood of this gathering, because no matter how much cajoling we gave her, she refused to smile. I remember her solemn little face and how we kidded to her by calling her 'little sobersides' but to no avail. She simply refused to smile for us, as if she had a presentiment of something bad about to happen to her. That photograph represented to everyone there that day my imminent departure from my husband, my children and my present life, plus it symbolised my dismal prospects for a very changed and uncertain future. Sadly, the photo seems to have disappeared, but the memory of that day lingers on for the both of us – mother and child.

Everything was done in a flurry of activity, and I remember the day I entered the Heatherton Sanatorium with Ron carrying my case of belongings and leaving me, forbidden to give me a farewell kiss because of the risk of contagion. I felt like a prisoner who had been given a death sentence for a crime I had not committed. It was very much the 'Why me?' factor at work. I wondered what I had done to deserve this dreaded disease when I had always seemed so fit and healthy. I did my utmost to appear calm, but beneath the surface, my heart was racing, and I felt an inevitable sensation of dread. I was ushered into a long ward of beds, already occupied by similarly affected females, some of whom appeared seriously unwell, with wasted bodies and pale, stretched features. We were situated on a veranda with fly-wire in place of glass windows, as the theory was that fresh air was essential. I dreaded the thought of remaining there for the Winter! Some were in a more serious state than others, lying back and propped up with pillows, but others were sitting up with knitting or books to occupy their time whilst trying to convalesce from this deadly disease which had taken a toll on so many before them. I was told to undress and don my nightgown before climbing into a bed already prepared and topped with a thick white, cotton cover the same as all the rest in the room. My belongings were placed in a small dresser beside the bed, and this was to be my life for what was the unforeseeable future. Apart from bed rest, it seemed that there was no particular treatment to enhance my prospects for a recovery, other than to spend as much time as possible sitting in a deck chair and absorbing the sunshine wherever possible. My husband, Ron, was permitted to visit me on a Sunday afternoon, but all other visitors were strictly forbidden, particularly my children.

My greatest concern was over what was to become of the children. I knew that they could enter an orphanage unless someone in the family undertook to care for them. Inevitably, it was my parents who came to the rescue, as neither of them could tolerate the prospect of placing their grandchildren in such a dreaded institution. After a period in hospital my son, William (later called Billy), recovered and was released into their care with the proviso that they all had regular six-monthly x-rays to check their progress. My mother, Evelyn, enjoyed caring for young children as she had previously worked as a nanny, and they adjusted quickly to her mollycoddling ways. An example of this was how, even when Billy was a toddler, Evelyn would load him into the baby pram and wheel him everywhere, as if he was still a baby, regardless of how ridiculous it looked. Sadly, Yvonne and Billy were so young that I realised, as their mother, I would soon become a distant stranger and almost a figment of their imagination. I was someone who occasionally sent a letter that was read to them, and the only tangible reminder of my existence were the felt toys that I learnt to make; these I sent home for each child as a gift from their absent mother. One particular favourite for Yvonne was a pretty Dutch girl doll and the other one that I made for Billy who carried it everywhere with him was a long- legged monkey with a long, curving tail, dressed in a monkey costume.

53. Billy with Monkey

Billy loved this particular toy, and many a joke was passed, because it was said that he actually looked and behaved like a little monkey due to his mischievous pranks and his cheeky smile. Sadly, as months turned into years, I became more resentful towards my mother, Evelyn, because I regarded her as stealing the affections of my children that were due to me as their real mother. With the prospect of endless days stuck in a hospital with no other option in sight, my outlook became rather distorted, and she bore the brunt of my frustrations. In hindsight, I realise that no matter what she did, she could never have been blameless in my eyes, due to the fact that our relationship as mother and daughter had never been adequately restored.

As if my parents did not have enough to cope with, another tragedy was about to befall them. Their daughter, Doris, had finished her schooling at the Methodist Ladies' College and gained employment at a local clothing factory. She had no aspirations to further her education, but displayed a creative talent for sewing and doing elaborate decorative handworks; a talent she may have inherited from her namesake, Auntie Doris. She enjoyed dressmaking and made many items of clothing. She had a gentle, giving personality and made many friends among her work mates. She had a certain beauty, with long, rich black hair and smooth olive skin, enhanced by large, dark eyes. Her figure was rounded and solid boned; not considered to be the slim ideal of fashionable womanhood perhaps, but nevertheless, in my eyes, she was exotically different and although circumstances had determined that we were not intimately close, I cared for her as my only sister. Whilst I was in hospital, Ron often brought me photos of the children and I remember feeling both proud and sadly deprived to see the photos of the occasion when my daughter, Yvonne, was a flower girl at the wedding of Eva, a close friend of Doris. She looked to be growing up so fast and she had her hair extra tightly curled for the occasion, wearing a lovely long white dress that Doris had made for her and carrying a bouquet of flowers.

54. Photo of Yvonne as Flower girl

It pained me to think that I was unable to have any contact with my daughter and the thought occurred to me that I may never get to see her again. It was not long after this event that Doris became quite ill. My mother and my stepfather, Hedley, were absolutely devastated when they were given the medical verdict that Doris had contracted tubercular meningitis on the brain and would need to be hospitalised immediately. She was sent to the Royal Melbourne for treatment, and my mother was frantic with worry about the health of her favourite daughter. The consequence of this terrible situation was the excessive burden it placed on my parents who had the care of my children while at the same time, both daughters were in hospital with deadly illnesses. To make matters worse, Hedley had earlier been transferred to Adelaide by the public service. I suspect that there were other marital reasons for him accepting or perhaps even applying for the transfer, which meant that the burden of care then fell completely upon my mother. Instead it was decided that young Billy and Yvonne should temporarily go to stay with my husband Ron's mother, Jessie Lidgerwood, at 12 Bowen Street, Hawthorn. She had a large double fronted Victorian house with a sleep-out added to the back and the right side of the front veranda had been converted into a bedroom for my husband Ron, who returned to live there after I entered the sanatorium. His mother ran a boarding house, renting some of the internal bedrooms and the rear sleep-out to individual boarders. Billy and Yvonne were to share a small, isolated room just off the dining room and kitchen at the rear of the house. They soon realised that they were not going to receive the spoiling they had become accustomed to with my own parents. Ron's mother had reluctantly agreed to take us in, but the children were very much left to their own devices. In many respects, they were made to feel just like the boarders who lived in the rest of the house; to be seen and not heard. Ron, their father, was physically separated from them at the front of the house and he was still a stranger to them more than a parent. There had not been the usual opportunities for bonding in the relationship, due to the war and continual separation from each other that they had experienced. Ron, strongly encouraged by his mother, was busy having a social life mostly as a single person, playing sport, going to dances and sharing time with his bachelor friend, Dougy. Since my hospitalization my young daughter, Yvonne, had become very protective towards her little three year old brother and she developed a heavy sense of responsibility as his big sister, which added a great deal of extra nervous stress, although she was then only six years of age.

They were both missing the company and care of Evelyn, their grandmother, and longing for the time when they could return to her. However, it seemed more and more unlikely as time passed by. The situation was finally compounded by an accidental event that occurred when Evelyn had been rushing between the two hospitals, visiting both Doris and Nancy and taking special food she had cooked to tempt their appetites. She was feeling exhausted when the tram pulled up in Barkers Road and she wearily stepped off onto the road without looking. She was knocked down by a car and taken to hospital by ambulance, having deeply cut her face and receiving a broken leg. She found herself immobilised in a hospital bed and on crutches for a considerable length of time afterwards. It was this occurrence that determined the end of Yvonne and Billy's time with their Nanna Way at Barkers Road. Life became very different for the children, and each day Billy would be taken by Grandma Jessie Lidgerwood daily to visit the home nearby of a wealthy local doctor where she had additional work as a housekeeper. Consequently, instead of attending the Methodist Ladies' College where she had been formerly enrolled to go when living at Barkers Road just like her Auntie Doris before her, Yvonne was enrolled in first grade at Auburn State School, which was a long walk from Bowen Street, Hawthorn, where she now lived. She was shown the way, and each day she was expected to walk the distance to school on her own. There were many times when she felt neglected, unloved and alone in the world and she longed to be back with her Nanna Way and Hedley. She still remembers the chilblains she developed all over her hands from the cold, wet mornings walking to school without gloves on her hands and the sopping wet hemline that developed on her rubber coated, pixie-hooded raincoat with the front slits for her hands to poke thru. It chafed and reddened her legs along the wet hemline. When she was in grade three, young Billy was also enrolled. He accompanied her on their daily walk to and from school. He was a bit of a handful because he was inclined to be rather mischievous and wilful by nature, but she did her best to look after him. However, one particular day, which stood clearly in her memory was when she was at school and summoned urgently to the headmaster's office. Billy was in the room, screaming loudly, with blood on his face and a cloth covering a deep gash on his head. He had been running up the rock slope of the sunken playground, which was out of bounds, and he had tripped and fallen, splitting his head open. Yvonne was expected to calm him while a taxi was called to take them home and get medical attention. Unfortunately, Yvonne was not much help because at the sight of her little brother in so much distress, she turned completely white-faced and fainted onto the floor. The outcome was that both children were sent home in the taxi and after Billy had medical attention for his wound, the two of them ended up in bed for the rest of the day, with a very displeased grandmother to keep an eye on them. Of course, the story of this event was later relayed to me when Ron was on his next Sunday visit to the 'Sana' to see me. I was upset and frustrated because I was completely helpless to get involved and do anything a mother would normally do.

SEPARATION & SORROW

On top of all the trauma which plagued our family's fortunes, it became apparent that my mother and Hedley were becoming more and more estranged from each other. Evelyn felt bitter about the way Hedley seemed to have abandoned her and left her with the heavy burden of attending to the continuing needs of both their daughters in hospital. It turned out that his recent transfer to Adelaide had occurred apparently, by accepting a promotion he had applied for. When Evelyn was informed that Doris was in remission and able to come home for a period, she was feeling exhausted and decided that she must have a break. Thinking that it was about time Hedley helped out, she contacted him in Adelaide to inform him that she was sending Doris to stay with him because she needed a holiday. Soon after, Doris was put on the Overland train and farewelled by her mother before the long rail journey she had ahead of her. Hedley was to meet her on her arrival, but when he collected her at the station Doris appeared rather exhausted from the journey and he became worried about her. The following day, she suffered a relapse and collapsed, falling into a coma. By the time she was taken to hospital her condition was no better and tragically, she never recovered consciousness. Hedley was traumatised and grief stricken to have lost his only biological daughter so young at only twenty years of age. He blamed Evelyn for sending her to him unaccompanied and when Evelyn heard the tragic news, she screamed in disbelief and her sorrow was inconsolable. She blamed Hedley for having abandoned them and leaving her on her own to deal with all the responsibility and the despair of watching their daughters held in such life-threatening circumstances. In hindsight, I recognise that she held such a deeply hidden remorse and guilt about sending Doris to Hedley in Adelaide that this catastrophic decision plagued her for the remainder of her days This was to be the irreparable final cause of their irreconcilable differences, with bitter accusations on both sides. Eventually the divorce papers arrived for my mother, Evelyn, to sign, but they were met with a point-blank refusal.

It was to be many years before Hedley was able to legally gain his freedom and marry Gladys who became his second wife. Sadly, there are now many gaps in the family photo albums of this era, as my mother removed all images of her and Hedley together, as if trying to erase all memories of the time they shared as a married couple.

In the ensuing years whilst I was still incarcerated at the sanatorium, with fellow patients dying like flies around me, Ron visited faithfully every Sunday without fail. I realised that I was extremely lucky that he continued to adore me, despite the fact that his mother encouraged him to go out to dances with his mate Dougy, whose father owned the local bakery down the corner of Bowen Street. Ron loved to dance, and I was aware that his mother was hoping that he would find someone else. After all, I wasn't expected to survive the tuberculosis, and I had already seen many other patients agonisingly pre-decease me, despite experiencing shorter periods of this illness. I cannot fully explain to someone who has not experienced this, just how it hardens the spirit and teaches one to tolerate the death of a fellow bed companion when it becomes such a regular consequence of being incarcerated together, year in and year out. Yes, I learnt to bury my feelings until it became second nature and a hardened part of my personality to 'tough things out' that never left me in the years to come.

At some stage, the x-rays revealed both lungs were so badly affected that it was decided to try collapsing those affected parts of each lung. It was an agonising experience because they inserted long needles right through into the lung cavities. It may have lengthened my life, but as the years advanced, it was unlikely that I would endure much longer as I was heading towards the five-year period that seemed equal to a prison sentence without end. Even now, I regard the following circumstances as a miracle! A new drug had recently been tested and it demonstrated incredible success in aiding the recovery of long-term tubercular patients like myself: it was known as Streptomycin. I was approached by doctors at Heatherton Sanatorium who were very familiar with my case, informing me of this news and asking me if I was prepared to become one of their 'guinea pigs' to test the effectiveness of this new drug. I jumped at this opportunity, because I had been gradually losing the will to fight this disease and felt myself to be losing the battle. I had already accepted that I was soon going to die as it had seemed inevitable.

Before long, I received the first of a series of treatments with this new drug and to the amazement of all, including myself, I began to improve, and the x-rays showed that the infection invading my lungs was beginning to dissipate. I was so excited to tell Ron such amazing good news on his Sunday visit. He had been so very anxious about me as he witnessed my decline, that he actually broke down and we cried together at this miraculous turn of fortune. For the very first time there was hope and we were able to look ahead and discuss possible plans for a future together and being a family again with our two children. I felt like I had been to hell and back! I remember the day when I was finally discharged and permitted to come home, with the proviso that I was to be regarded as a semi-invalid. I was told that it would be inadvisable to contemplate having any more children. Ron came to collect me, still in my dressing gown. We arrived by taxi at his mother's house in Bowen Street, and when the taxi pulled up, I was met by a gathering out front: his mother and father, brother Archie, and our children Yvonne and Billy who were eagerly awaiting this mystery mother they had no memory of to arrive. Yvonne held back shyly at first, but when I came through the front gate, she suddenly rushed towards me, crying, 'Mummy, welcome home!' She had taken me by surprise and when she reached up on tiptoe to kiss me, I automatically reached out with my hand to prevent her, saying 'I am not allowed to kiss anyone'. She immediately stepped back with a hurt expression, which turned into a blank and defensive look. I realised that she felt rejected, but at the time I was unable to deal with my emotions and ill equipped to become the doting, affectionate fairy godmother, a fantasy figure that she had imagined over the past five years of our separation. I had become emotionally hardened over this period and she was no longer my spoilt little girl of three years old. Sadly, the close bonds had been severed between us and over time they never really healed. So it became difficult for either of us to communicate any true affection or discuss how we felt, other than go through the motions of living and everyday elements of conversation. We had become permanently distanced from one another as mother and child. It occurs to me now, how strangely history has repeated itself, thinking of my dysfunctional relationship with Evelyn, my own mother.

The next shock came when I received word from my stepfather, Hedley, via a letter that he was seeking a divorce. As an afterthought, it came to me as not so surprising, as they shared little in common and had grown apart over the years. I had long realised that my stepfather was not happy in their relationship but put up with it as best he could. He wrote to explain that, with the death of their daughter, Doris, he felt that they had no longer anything in common to hold their marriage together. Whilst in Adelaide, he had met a woman named Gladys; he enjoyed her company and he wanted to marry her when a divorce came through. My mother became extremely angry and, on the grounds of being a Catholic, she refused to give him a divorce under any circumstances. She was extremely bitter and destroyed all family photographs which contained an image of Hedley. My mother told me I was to have nothing more to do with him, but I received a final letter from him, sending me some money and trying to explain that there was nothing left between him and my mother, and hoping he could have a new life with some happiness. I was very sad to be losing my dear stepfather, but understood the emptiness he felt within the marriage, where they had grown apart irreparably. The death of my half-sister, Doris, was the final, separating blow. Hedley arranged and covered all costs of the funeral, which took place in Adelaide, and my mother felt unwelcome to attend. She was mentally distraught in the knowledge that she had no claim or financial control over the burial and where Doris was set to rest in a grave legally owned by Hedley at the Centennial Cemetery in Adelaide. She travelled over to visit the grave shortly afterwards, but in an emotionally distraught state: before returning home, she burst into Hedley's office one weekday and made an embarrassing scene, screaming accusations at the top of her voice with no regard for his shocked office companions as he made his escape to another room. She was politely asked to leave, and guided to the door, never to see or speak with Hedley again. I wrote a final letter to Hedley, my stepfather, thanking him for the gift of money and regretfully wishing him a new and happier life. I determined at that time, that he had a right to be free of any further retribution by my mother, and undertook to free him of any further obligations to me or my own family. In effect, it was to be my goodbye, because I realised that I must support my own mother and let go of him, although he was the only father I had ever known. Thus, Hedley continued with his new life in Adelaide and eventually he was legally able to marry Gladys, despite the uncooperativeness of my mother.

55. Photo of Gladys and Hedley

Unfortunately, the abandonment of his marriage to Evelyn created a huge rift with his own family in Ballarat, as it went totally against the Christian principles of Hedley's father, Reverend John Tong Way. He was virtually cast out and condemned for his failure to support my mother after the death of Doris, and no member of the Tong Way family maintained any more contact with him or his second wife, whom they never met. From that time, Evelyn, my mother, began her annual pilgrimages by train from Melbourne to Adelaide to visit the grave of her beloved daughter, Doris, almost up until her death at age 85 in 1984. She often took my daughter, Yvonne, with her for company and it was Yvonne who related many of the events that took place. The sad consequence of all this was my loss of a stepfather, but also the tragic loss of a beloved grandfather for my two young children who never saw him again. It was particularly hard for Yvonne as the eldest child who, at nine years of age, missed him very much and could not understand why she was unable to see him ever again.

The epitaph to my story is that time was unable to heal the rifts in our family, created by circumstances largely beyond our control.

Yvonne was never able to completely accept the loss of her grandfather. As my eldest child, she was the one who remembered our Chinese links as a family: the visits to Ballarat in Hedley's old Austin 7 to see her elderly, Chinese great grandfather at the Young Street manse, and the occasions when the Chinese side of the family got together for meals cooked by John Tong Way and Uncle Joe, his eldest son. She always remembered how she loved the steamed bread that was served up at breakfast, plastered with butter and vegemite, plus the steaming bowls of Chinese food with fresh vegetables, cooked and picked straight from the garden and eaten with chopsticks around the large table where one could help oneself. On their last visit, naughty Billy threw great grandfather's broom up on the shed roof, much to the old man's consternation before Hedley was able to fetch it down. These are the glimpses of special moments that have stuck with Yvonne all these years ago. After John Tong Way retired in 1949, the Presbyterian Church had the wooden Chinese mission church building removed and relocated from the land adjoining the manse to serve a new purpose. Thus, a lifetime of dedicated work for the Ballarat Chinese came to a final end. The Reverend moved in retirement to be with his eldest son, Joseph, in East Melbourne, and after the death of Joe in 1957 he spent his final years living in the care of his daughter, Doris, in Castlemaine where he died in 1960 at the remarkable age of 100 years. He was buried with his wife, Mary, who pre-deceased him in 1941. They rest together in the Presbyterian section of the New Ballarat Cemetery, with this final epitaph inscribed upon the tombstone:

'Blessed are they who die in the Lord.'

THE GRANDDAUGHTER'S FINAL WORD

I never fully accepted the loss of my grandfather Hedley Way, and I lived for many years with the notion that there was always something missing and not fully resolved. The fact that I did not know Hedley's whereabouts or was never able to get in touch with him sometimes troubled me, even after so many decades of silence. During the past, in answer to my questions, my mother, Nancy, had told me, 'He is no longer your grandfather, and we have to let him go, so he is able to make a new life'. She explained that she did not make any further effort to contact Hedley because she felt this was the kindest thing to do, due to her mother's ongoing bitterness. The years rolled by, with the question of Hedley's whereabouts unanswered. Much later on, as an adult with a young family of my own, I finally decided to try and trace his whereabouts by visiting the grave of my mother's sister, my aunt Doris, at the Centennial Park Cemetery in Adelaide. When I found the grave, I was quite shocked and overcome with emotion to discover that it was too late! Hedley had died several years earlier, before my visit there in 1986. He was laid to rest with his daughter, Doris Winifred Way, his only biological child who had passed away so tragically decades ago at just twenty years of age. As the tears filled my eyes and numbed my heart, it was a moment of deep regret for me, in the realisation that I had left it too late to reconnect with my long-lost grandfather.

It was this bitter realisation that finally drove me to enquire at the cemetery office to see if I could find out who owned rights to the grave site, wondering if Hedley's wife, Gladys, may still be alive. I introduced myself as a relative and, thankfully, I was given the address of Gladys Way, who now held the legal rights over the grave as Hedley's beneficiary. When I found the correct house, I plucked up the courage to knock on the door. It opened to reveal an elderly lady of slim build, greying hair, and she was slightly stooped. She obviously had no recognition of this newcomer who had come to her door. My heart was racing as I nervously said, 'You do not know me, but I am the granddaughter of your husband, Hedley, from his first marriage. I have come over on a visit from Ballarat where I live, and I have just been to visit your husband's grave. It was a shock to discover that I am too late to meet him again and I am feeling so sad about it. I hope you do not mind me calling to introduce myself'. Although she looked surprised and she was obviously taken aback, she kindly invited me to come in and said, 'He often wondered why your mother, Nancy, never got in touch with him again, but he was very upset with the way your grandmother behaved when they parted'. I agreed that it was a very bitter parting, and apologised on behalf of my grandmother. Gladys graciously responded by saying, 'It is not your fault, dear; a lot of water has gone under the bridge since then'. She seemed to be pleased to make my acquaintance, perhaps because it was my connection with Hedley's earlier life. I looked about the room and it was with a strange stirring of memory and emotion that I observed the beautiful ceramic Buddha placed centrally on the sideboard. I immediately recalled it as the one which had sat on my grandmother's own sideboard many years ago when it was a treasured possession of Hedley's. It was, of course, something he would have insisted on taking with him. At this moment for me, it represented a symbol of our family's loss and a recognition that it was an emblem of the past for which we had no further claim. It was, in many ways, an emotional meeting for us both and, to my relief, we parted warmly.

When I returned to Ballarat, I decided to write to Gladys and try to develop some ongoing contact with her, hoping to find out more about Hedley's life with her. It was the only connection I could maintain, and it was with pleasure that I received a reply letter. This was the beginning of getting to know each other by mail and we developed an ongoing friendship over the next years, when I learnt more about her and her family life with Hedley. In return, I shared with her the few special memories I had of my times with Hedley as my beloved grandfather – the trips to Ballarat to see his ageing father, travelling in the 'flea' that was the Austin 7, crammed from floor almost to ceiling with luggage, the four of us, plus even the cat on board. I remember that, halfway there, the car overheated, and we were forced to stop and disembark at Djerriwah Creek which was a steep climb down from the road, in order to fill the radiator with a container of water before we could continue the journey. In those days, the trip took much longer along the narrow, winding road compared with the freeway of today. Also, there was the trip and holiday in Torquay with my grandparents and I remember how Hedley loved to go rabbiting. He had set some traps and brought back this rabbit with a broken leg at which my Nanna berated him angrily for his cruelty in making the animal suffer. Being a country girl, she demonstrated her skills by creeping up on a tussock of grass and grabbing it with both hands and to our astonishment, holding up a rabbit by its ears. However, my fondest memory is of the times when my grandfather was playing his violin upstairs in the Barkers Road home and I was able to share time with him alone, just listening and learning to share his appreciation of the music.

Meanwhile, I was faced with the declining health of my grandmother

Evelyn, who developed Parkinson's Disease: she eventually became wheelchair-bound and helpless to look after herself properly. Because there existed no close mother and daughter relationship between my mother and grandmother, I became the one my grandmother trusted to carry out her wishes and act on her behalf. I found this difficult, because I realised that it would further complicate my relationship with my mother. However, although conflicted, I could not deny the love Nanna had always given me unconditionally. Now married, with a family of my own, I was summoned to discuss her wishes for the future. She made it very clear that when she died, she wished to be buried in Adelaide along with her beloved daughter, Doris. I explained that this was a difficult request because Hedley was now buried with her and the grave now legally belonged to Hedley's wife, Gladys, who eventually intended to be buried with him in the same plot. Shortly afterwards, I arranged to see Nanna's doctor and discussed with him the best option for my grandmother's care. Arrangements were made for Nanna to enter permanent care in an old people's home not that far from her house in Thornbury. There was really no other option at this stage, despite great reluctance on Nanna's part. She always referred to it as 'the morgue' and was not a very happy or co-operative patient. My own family found it was distressing to visit her on the many long trips down from Ballarat where we then lived, and we witnessed her declining rapidly. She had always provided a haven of love and protection for me and my brother Billy. Nanna's place provided the blanket of security, even when we grew up and had our own lives to live. Therefore, on one of my last visits to see my failing, beloved grandmother, I made a promise to her that I would do my utmost to carry out her final, dearest wish that she had frequently expressed: to be buried with her beloved daughter, Doris. 'I will do everything I can, Nanna,' I said. 'I know how much it means to you.' The truth was that, in my heart I was doubtful about whether I would ever be able to keep my promise, but I wanted her at peace and did not wish to upset her with these considerations.

Shortly afterwards, when Nanna died, she was cremated, and I had the dilemma of how I would be able to keep my promise. I decided that I would keep Nanna's ashes with me in the camphorwood box she had left to me in the hope that something could be resolved. With trepidation, I wrote to Gladys, advising her of my grandmother's death and I tried to explain the situation. I asked if Gladys would permit my grandmother's last wish for her ashes to be buried with her daughter and finally let bygones be bygones, overlooking the bitterness of the past. It was a difficult letter to write, with a great deal of apprehension about the reply. However, it was not long before I received a gracious note from Gladys, agreeing for me to arrange the placement of Nanna's ashes in the grave, with a bronze plaque attached to the base of the tombstone. I was so relieved and appreciative of her understanding and generosity, which had eventuated because of the ongoing friendship we had formed. It had been the nearest I would ever come to my grandfather again and it allowed me to consider myself somehow more connected than before. A visit to Adelaide and the cemetery was pre-arranged. A brass plaque had been ordered and the cemetery had organised for a hollow to be dug in readiness at the base of the tombstone. With tears falling down my face and a lump in my throat, it was an emotional moment when I knelt and placed Nanna's ashes gently into the prepared spot. The final words I had arranged to be engraved on the plaque, I read out aloud in a trembling voice:

'Together at Last'

56. Hedley & Doris' grave and Evelyn's plaque

In a strangely symbolic way, it was a moment of reconnection and healing, a removal of the years of bitterness, recrimination and regret. I felt vindicated on behalf of both my grandfather and my grandmother. I knew that I had done my utmost to keep faith with my grandmother's deepest wish. In doing so, I had become the catalyst to try and heal the scars of heartbreak and loss from over thirty-five years ago.

CHINESE AUNT (TO DORIS)

How come,
Half-caste oriental,
You were my Aunt?

You're just a picture on the sideboard now,
We know each other well,
Our eyes together leave this room;
We seek to bury a mother's grief,
Borne in burying you.

I your step-niece,
You, with jet black mane,
Body full substanced
And of generous proportion
With whom a question unanswered
Still lingers …

Your soft voice sounding
A dead echo from sensuous lips,
Brown depths unfathomable
Dwell in the limitless pools of your eyes.

Enclosed by a picture frame,
You live falsely cut off
From the taint
Of an alien ancestry,
Half-caste oriental,
You were never to be
A joiner of two worlds;
Suffice it to say,
'the good die young!'

By Yvonne Horsfield

FIRST RECOLLECTIONS

'Smile for your picture
Little Sobersides'
they chided.

On this special occasion
I was closeted with relatives.
Bedecked in Sunday Best:
Hatless Aunts in pre-war outfits,
Pin-striped Uncles, steamed and pressed,
It was a holiday for mothballs
at the families' request.

'Smile for your picture
and watch the little birdie!'
Their adult minds were orphaning
my three years of age,
Glacier grins in rigid frames,
Their eyes held secret information.
(Your mother is consumptive,
so smile before she dies!)

I watched the hooded blackness
of the box.
Freezing time and cloying relatives,
as peaches in preservative,
We sepia-toned a moment,
We lingered with last lies,
Casting memories on cardboard
in a coffin-like request
to know the colour of her eyes.

By Yvonne Horsfield

LIST OF ILLUSTRATIONS

Contents Page

Family tree *(Compiled by Linton Horsfield)*

Tsin Chin Shan – First Generation

1. Line drawing of Chinese *(drawing by Garth Horsfield)*

2. Photo of village - Wang Tung 2018 *(photo by Yvonne Horsfield)*

Second Generation Gold Seeker

3. Rev. James Chue *(Tong Way family collection)*

4. Lo Kwoi Sang *(Loh, Morag - old photo)*

5. Reverend William Youngman and wife *("Soldiers & Settlers: Chinese in Victoria")*

The Mining of Souls

6. Photo of early Nerrina (Little Bendigo) *(Creswick Museum booklet - "Spirit of China" (old photo))*

7. Site of old Black Hill Diggings *(Photo-Australiana Collection. Ballarat Library)*

8. St Andrews Kirk (Recent) *(photo by Linton Horsfield)*

9. Ship "Airlie" photo *(photo online. State Library of Queensland)*

Parental Decision

10. Bethesda Lutheran Orphanage photo *(photo online. State Library of Queensland)*

11. Brown Hill State School *(photo online. Brown Hill Progress Ass'n)*

12. Mary's Chinese wedding outfit *(Tong Way family collection)*

13 Tong Wai and Quong - double wedding *(Tong Way family collection)*

14. Photo of Quong family *(Family collection of Noela Bull)*

Life at 6 Young Street

15. Church and Manse Young St *(Tong Way family collection)*

16. Golden Point State School

17. Ballarat Agricultural High School (old) *(online, courtesy Public Records)*

18. Humffray St. School *(online, courtesy Public Records)*

19. Rare photo of Gladys (centre) surrounded by family *(Tong Way family collection)*

20. 31 Barkly St. - Stanhope house *(photo provided by Stanhope family)*

21. Photo Miss Booth & Mrs Stanhope *(photo provided by Stanhope family)*

22. Photo of Ballarat Joss house 1955 *(provided by Sovereign Hill archives)*

The Tragedy of Loss

23. Photo of Kenneth Tong Wai *(Tong Way family collection)*

The War Years Intervened

24. Hedley and Sam in uniform *(Tong Way family collection)*

25. Photo of Hedley and William Watkins *(Tong Way family collection)*

26. Photo of Sam Tongway's graduation *(Tong Way family collection)*

27. Photo of Sam's avenue tree and plaque *(Tong Way family collection)*

28. ANA membership certificate photo *(Provided by Sam Tongway)*

New Challenges for the Family

29. John and Mary photos (Headshots) *(Tong Way family collection)*

30. Alien application form for Mary *(National Archives Australia)*

31. Photo of young Nancy and mother Evelyn *(Nancy Way collection (Yvonne's mother))*

32. Photo - Baby Doris & father Hedley *(Nancy Way collection (Yvonne's mother))*

33. Photo of Joseph Tong Wai (enlargement from certificate) *(National Archives Australia)*

34. Joseph's Alien Certificate *(National Archives Australia))*

Third-Generation Chinese-Australian Citizens

35. Photo of Sam as Principal *(provided by Sam Tongway)*

36. Rare family group photo (Hedley, back row, 2nd row L-R Evelyn & Ken, 3rd row L-R Vi, Sam & Nancy with baby Doris & Aunt Doris) *(Nancy Way collection)*

37. Photo of Sam at bowls *(provided by Sam Tongway)*

38. Photo of Doris *(Nancy Way collection)*

39. Doris' artwork *(Newstead Museum collection)*

40. Doris at writing desk *(Newstead Museum collection)*

41. Excerpt letter former pupil *(Newstead Museum collection)*

42. Photo of John Tong Way's grave *(photo by Yvonne Horsfield)*

The End of an Era

43. Photo of sign at 6 Young St *(photo by Yvonne Horsfield)*

44. Michael Way & new monument *(photo by Yvonne Horsfield)*

Nancy's Own Story

45. Photo of Baby Doris with Evelyn *(Nancy Way collection)*

46. Photo of young Doris, 1936, L-R, 5th in centre row *(Nancy Way collection)*

47. St Johns Presbyterian Church *(photo online)*

48. Nancy and sister Doris Way *(Nancy Way collection)*

49. Methodists Ladies College *(photo online)*

50. RAAF photo of Ron *(Yvonne's family collection)*

51. Aunty "Vonnie" nursing Doris *(Nancy Way collection)*

52. Heatherton Sanitarium *(photo online)*

53. Billy with Monkey *(Nancy Way collection)*

54. Photo of Yvonne as flower girl *(Nancy Way collection)*

55. Photo of Gladys and Hedley *(photo provided by Gladys Way, 2nd wife)*

56. Hedley & Doris' grave and Evelyn's plaque *(photo by Yvonne)*

Poems

CHINESE AUNT (To Doris) *(written by Yvonne Horsfield)*

FIRST RECOLLECTIONS. (Sobersides) *(written by Yvonne Horsfield)*

Please note: The majority of photos (including those sourced online) are excempt from the copyright law restrictions as being beyond 50 years. Any other sources have been acknowledged to the best of my ability. Yvonne Horsfield

Shawline Publishing Group Pty Ltd
www.shawlinepublishing.com.au

More great Shawline titles can be found here

New titles also available through Books@Home Pty Ltd.
Subscribe today - www.booksathome.com.au

Ingram Content Group UK Ltd.
Milton Keynes UK
UKHW020803270323
419227UK00016B/920